BodyTalk
at Work

D1347277

BodyTalk
at Work

How to Use Effective Body Language to Boost Your Career

JUDI JAMES

PIATKUS

First published in 2001 by
Judy Piatkus (Publishers) Limited
5 Windmill Street
London W1T 2JA
e-mail: info@piatkus.co.uk

This paperback edition published in 2001

The moral right of the author has been asserted
A catalogue record for this book is available from the British Library
ISBN 0–7499–2192–7 Hbk
ISBN 0–7499–2258–3 Pbk

This book has been printed on paper manufactured with respect for the
environment using wood from managed sustainable resources

Text design by Paul Saunders

Data capture and manipulation by
Phoenix Photosetting, Chatham, Kent
Printed and bound in Great Britain by
Mackays of Chatham, Kent

Contents

What is Bodytalk?

BODYTALK IS PART of every transaction in the workplace. It governs how we communicate and work with others. It is a major part of our personal career success.

My interest in body language started when I was coaching people to be more effective at recruitment interviews. By monitoring their non-verbal signals and then hearing the interviewers' responses to them I saw what a vital ingredient bodytalk could be in all business success. I now coach individuals and companies in this fascinating, funny, complex and largely misunderstood subject.

One thing I love about business people is their bravery. Actors learn to act. Singers train for years before they get up on stage. Yet corporate types are expected to present, sell, market themselves and generally perform with little or no training. There is a need for information that is up to date and yet down to earth, a guide for busy people, something quick-fix but comprehensive. That's why I wrote this book.

Let's Start Work . . .

Your job sets up daily challenges for your non-verbal signalling systems. On the one hand you will be coping with tribal and animal responses as old as mankind. On the other there is the need for a fast-track evolutionary process. Your ancestors didn't have to struggle with open-plan offices, video-conferencing, dress-down culture, Power Point presentations and gesture-jargon.

And then there is the constant demand for Academy award-style acting. Lying in the workplace may be subtle or overt, but it is there. Whatever our true feelings, we are required to love our job, respect our boss and feel passionate about our customers. So we learn to manage our natural responses. This form of masking may be 'civilised' behaviour, but it also destroys understanding.

One of the biggest problems in any business is lack of communication. Employees feel out of touch with high-level change. Managers fail to brief. Corporate goals are unclear. Departments fail to communicate with one another. And when we do speak we fail to understand the message.

As if this weren't enough, the longer working day has also led to relationship boundary-blurring. Not only do we go to work to earn money, but also to find friendship and even sex.

So, how can this book help you through the corporate minefield?

How to Use the Book

Bodytalk can be used in three ways and so can this book:

1. You can study your own non-verbal signals and modify them to make yourself more effective at self-marketing and communication in the workplace.

2. You can improve your skills of reading and understanding others.

3. You can begin to take control of your business transactions, looking at gaining control of specific workplace situations like meetings, sales presentations or front-line client communications.

Don't feel you have to read this book from cover to cover in one sitting. It has been written for people who are busy. You can use it on the hoof by dipping into chapters dealing with specific work situations or you can read the first section more thoroughly for long-term improvement.

Not all the change suggested will be long term. There are plenty of quick-fix techniques as well. Just remember one thing – you do need to start by feeling good about the product you are trying to market. That product is you.

How Body Language Works

In a sense, we are all experts on body language already. The survival instinct alone ensures we can read danger from others via visual signals. Babies, dogs and small children are adept at interpreting these complex messages, but as adults we underestimate this inborn skill. Yet even in a 'safe' environment like an office or meeting room you will feel a pull on your gaze each time someone new enters the room. And whether you want to or not, you will start to form opinions about a person in as little as three seconds.

You can try to be fair and objective in your evaluation, but you will have little choice. This is an area where the subconscious mind bullies the conscious into submission. Like, dislike, trust, love or lust can all be promoted in as long as it takes to clear your throat. In fact, most of these responses will be based on your perception of how the person looks. Various aspects of a person's appearance will trigger past experiences and emotional responses that you will use as a point of reference when dealing with similar-looking signals. So your brain will rifle through a variety of prejudicial stereotypes in a matter of seconds. This is the mental equivalent of rooting through a great stack of holiday baggage for something small you packed early on, near the bottom.

However, your conscious mind is aware that most of these visual signals can be, as we say in the trade, well dodgy. There are many reasons for this, especially in the workplace. Unlike other animals, humans constantly mask their unpleasant characteristics and are quite capable of looking friendly while stabbing you in the back. Wouldn't life be easier if all the baddies displayed themselves like the pantomime villain, hissing and grimacing as they tried to stitch you up on a deal?

The point is, people often do offer visual clues to what's going on behind the mask. OK, maybe not the manic eyes, demonic laughter or overt moustache-twiddling, but subtle stuff that emerges as what's called 'leakage'. Few people can act honest all the time, not even politicians and car salesmen. So, if you want a more accurate reading of the people you work and do business with, it's up to you to look out for the signals.

First Impressions

In business your communications and meetings with clients and colleagues may be fleeting. You may only have a few short seconds to decipher the true mood of the person you are dealing with, so that you can tailor your own response accordingly. The first impression, then, that great lifestyle cliché, can stand between you and success in business interviews, promotion, presentations, meetings, sales pitches and customer management. Before you kick off into the realms of self-improvement you need to know exactly how this first impression is created.

Fifty-five per cent of the perceived impact of communicated messages comes from non-verbal signals. And when verbal and visual communications are in conflict, it is the visual 'words' that people remember longer and find easier to trust.

The danger is, your subconscious tends to override open-minded fairness and non-judgemental thinking. Should you trust your finances to a man wearing a Mickey Mouse tie? What about that tattoo on the forearm of that woman you were interviewing? Better beware of that person who looks a bit like your old school bully. . .

Prejudiced though your subconscious can be, it rarely picks up on just one gesture. Instead it feeds on a whole mix of messages, known as 'cluster signals'. Next time you meet someone new, spend time working out what you thought of them when you first saw them. If you find it easier, you can do this experiment using a photo from a magazine. The logical part of your brain will probably tell you that you kept a completely open mind. But what about the emotional part? What were those first knee-jerk assumptions? Analyse where those responses came from. What was it about the person's appearance that stimulated those first feelings?

If you were to write a list, it would probably include their eye contact and gaze, facial expression, gestures, posture, vocal tone, spatial behaviour, touch, grooming and dress. These all make up our individual bodytalk.

Creating the 'Sight Bite'

Image in business, then, can make the difference between win and lose. Most careers involve constant and frequent first-impression communication and negotiation. Most businesses are performed on an ever-widening stage and that platform is set to grow even larger since the introduction of the great god globalisation.

So, your image is one of the most potent marketing tools at your disposal and your body language forms a vast part of that projected image. It is the tie-breaker in political elections, the clincher in a sale, the charisma in your communications. Good body language creates impact and empathy. The bad stuff can make you unpopular and unsuccessful throughout your entire career. And unfortunately you'd probably never know why you were jinxed. The problem is we don't get to see ourselves in action enough. You think you're doing OK. Then you catch a glimpse of yourself on video and the terrible truth begins to dawn . . .

Don't worry. This book will help you 'talk' better with your own body and learning to modify your own signals will enhance your skills of persuading and influencing, as well as lead to increased confidence and self-esteem and business success. Simply forget the 'trickery' and conventional wisdom of body language lore and relish the subtlety and intricacy of all our ways of communication.

Key Points in a Nutshell

▶ Understanding bodytalk is the key to business success.

▶ You will be working in three stages:

- tweaking your own bodytalk signals
- 'ear listening' – studying those of others
- 'corporate choreography' – taking control of workplace interactions

▶ Initial judgements are based on old stereotypes and prejudices. But you can get past them.

▶ Bodytalk will enable you to understand other people better and communicate more effectively, leading to increased self-esteem and success.

PART 1

How to be Your Own Spin Doctor – Improving Your Bodytalk

Chapter 1

_A_ssessing Your Current Image

SPIN-DOCTORING IS a hideous but necessary part of modern business life. People who either want to get jobs or to get on in jobs are having to launch themselves into a campaign of aggressive self-sell.

Unfortunately, rewards in work now come to those with a high profile, rather than those who deserve to do well. Seventy-two per cent of jobs go to people who interview effectively, rather than those who are suitable candidates.

Also, promotion is no longer a matter of filling 'dead man's shoes'. Career trails that used to be plodding and virtually inevitable are now erratic. There is almost no such thing as a 'steady' job. Even if you build a solid reputation in one company the current trend for mergers and takeovers can mean you will be starting from scratch when new bosses arrive. Qualities that may have been seen as laudable in the first firm can easily be viewed as negative by the new regime. 'Carl has worked here for years and is a loyal and valuable employee' may just sound like 'stick-in-the-mud who will be resistant to change'.

Whatever your situation, it's important to raise your profile.

▶ Change Management

Change as a culture is here to stay. The two largest cultural revolutions at work have been the open-plan office system and the introduction of IT. Both have led to massive changes in our communication styles. While we have become permanently visible via the first, the latter has eroded our verbal skills, with employees generally preferring e-mail and fax to face-to-face meetings.

In many firms spoken communication has been reduced to the level of jargon, business cliché, psycho-babble and computer geek-speak. In recent years we have seen the introduction of the 'can-do' culture, the 'no-blame' culture, the 'zero-error' culture, the 'get it right first time' culture and the 'customer-focus' culture. But few people believe that sort of rehearsed patter any more. We need a more meaningful form of communication.

Also, despite touchy-feely claims for the reverse, employees are still expected to live for work. In fact business life has made greater and grosser inroads into home and out-of-hours life with the introduction of mobiles, laptops and home-working options. So, not only do you have to sell yourself in the workplace, but you have to do it more often.

The Human Touch

Since the recent trend for companies to pare their staff to the bone in acts of feral restructuring, the emphasis has been on honing products and services to be competitive in a global marketplace. The human touch has been assumed to be *passé*. People would prefer to do business with machines: shopping, banking and even meeting their partners and friends via the Internet.

When products and prices begin to blur, though, it is the human face that makes the sale. We like 'characters', no matter how flawed. In our search for the person behind the product we will even make heroes out of characterless pop and sports stars and reticent royals. So, instead of hiding behind the new technology, staff are increasingly being winkled out and forced to stand centre-stage to impress internally and externally. Whether you like it or not, then, you are still the most valuable commodity in your company's business success.

To succeed at all, you need to sell yourself.

You have to do it yourself, too. Don't expect others to do this self-sell for you. Colleagues will rarely boast about you because they're competing. Bosses tend to keep good staff to themselves in case they get spirited away by promotion. You could end up the best-kept secret the company has. Is that what you want from your career?

▶ The Challenge of Change

Before you begin your self-marketing campaign, however, you need to be clear about three basic points:

1. You are on the wrong side of your eyeballs.

You make assumptions about the way you look and come across based on:

▶ the way you feel living inside your body

▶ comments others have made about your appearance over the years

▶ a few holiday snapshots

▶ the reflection you see each morning in a small mirror in the bathroom.

All this can only add up to one thing: you are deluded about your own appearance.

2. You will need to focus on the dos, not the don'ts.

Telling yourself what *not* to do never works (except in reverse), especially when you are training yourself out of bad body language habits. Focusing on *not* stuffing your hands in your pockets during a business presentation will only make you do it all the more. The subconscious mind eliminates the word 'don't' from commands it receives from the conscious mind and all it hears is the stimulus word. So 'Don't fiddle!' becomes a suggestion to do just that. Instead, tell yourself what you *do* want to do and how you *do* want to look.

3. It hurts.

Change can be painful. If you don't believe me, try this test. Next time you are happily chatting with someone at a social event, try telling them you are making a study of people's body language. Then stand back and watch them squirm. Being monitored is enough to make most people feel awkward and staring at someone can even provoke violence. 'Who're you looking at?' has launched countless drunken scuffles.

Self-watching is something else again. If someone else looks at you, you can at least walk out of their sight, but monitoring your own image means there's little in the way of a hiding-place.

Comfort Zones

Everyone likes to do things they know they're good at. That means we tend to spend quite a generous chunk of our lives inside a 'comfort zone', doing things we know we can do. This is what's called 'confidence' and what some may even call 'a mind-numbingly boring existence'.

Emerging from this zone of known ability means you will start to feel 'the stretch'. How does that one go? As an experiment, try folding your arms the wrong way round. How does it feel? Awkward? What do you most want to do next? Change them back because you know it will feel comfortable again?

Humans aren't stupid. When something makes us uncomfortable we crawl back into the nest. Avoid discomfort at all costs. Apart from Arctic explorers and those people who volunteer for outward-bound courses, that is. But for the rest of us, warm pub vs raft made of plastic cola bottles on icy river is a bit of a no-contest scenario.

Unnatural arm folding might not be the greatest goal of your life, but you can take my word for it that with dogged persistence your body would learn the new arm fold in about eight weeks. That's roughly how long it takes to learn a new habit or unlearn an old one. The same is true of changing a taste, like switching to tea without the sugar. Twelve cups should do it.

Forget the cola-bottle raft, though. The only discomfort you're going to have to move through to improve your bodytalk is a touch of physical awkwardness. A bit of clumsiness, maybe. Nothing painful. Nothing life-threatening.

The Way Ahead

Here's the entire spectrum of image change and how you will feel throughout the process, just so you can't say I didn't warn you beforehand:

The first stage you go through when modifying your body language is that happy state known as 'unconscious incompetence'. This is the stage when everyone else is aware of your annoying or negative habits, but you are in blissful ignorance.

Then someone either buys you this book or you are forced to watch yourself on a workplace video. This experience catapults you on to the second stage of the self-discovery and learning trail, known as 'conscious incompetence'. Horrified, you vow never to show your face in public again. Hence the first pain-barrier, induced by the rawness of self-discovery.

At this stage you have one of three options:

1. Go into denial, claiming the video was doctored or the book is full of claptrap.

2. Try to forget the whole experience and return to the 'ignorance is bliss' state.

3. Work on improving your body language.

Guess which option is the most difficult? And guess which will be the most rewarding ultimately?

Once you decide to select the 'improvement' option, what happens next is you try to change what you are doing. There will be a comical aspect to this vital stage, but don't expect it to be you who finds it funny.

Over-correction tends to be the order of the day as you turn overt arm movements into something resembling a penguin in splints. The wide smile becomes a puckered prune and the hesitant eye contact is swapped for a manic stare. This type of over-correction is known as 'pin-balling', veering from one extreme to another in a desire to correct.

This is, of course, exquisitely painful. The gestures and expressions feel alien. They are not yet part of your normal body choreography. You feel like a prize turnip and probably look a bit like one, as well. It would be easy to quit but also a pity. You have come too far to go back. The last stage is a mere whisper away. Really.

This stage is the one you're least likely to recognise. It's when the pain starts to stop and the better bodytalk begins. It is 'unconscious competence'. You'll barely notice it's happened. Not noticing is part of the process. And it *will* happen. The body will just take over and do it for you. You've been practising for so long the responses will become automatic, which is why this is called 'muscle memory'. The positive gestures and expressions have become absorbed into your normal routine and suddenly you don't feel quite so silly or self-conscious about them any more.

Navel-gazing

One brief exercise, then, before you get into action, one small but necessary spot of self-assessment. Take a large sheet of paper and a pen. Now answer the following three questions:

1. Describe your current business image. How do you think you come across at work? How would your colleagues/boss/employees/customers describe you?

2. How would you *like* to come across? What is your ideal image?

3. Now evaluate your inner image. Describe your feelings during the working day. Are you confident? Relaxed? Paranoid? Bored? Stimulated? Stressed?

That may not have been easy, but this basic exercise is a vital step to self-improvement. You need to study the raw material to know what it is you are working with. This is the stage where you get the plasticine out of the packet and examine it before using it to make another shape. What colour is it? What shape is it already? How does it feel? What would it like to be? Mould it around for a bit. Now prepare to roll up your sleeves and get stuck in. You're going to be modelling a new and successful you.

The Image M.O.T.

Tinkering around with your business image can lead to incongruent signalling, though. This is where the picture doesn't work. You may, for example, choose to mask your inner insecurities or nervousness with an outward display of confidence, or attempt to show friendliness towards a client you would prefer to see die slowly and painfully. Such 'masking' is an essential part of workplace behaviour. But if it appears insincere, people will assume you lack integrity and not trust you at all.

If your masking is to work, you will need to fool all of the people all of the time, including possibly yourself. If you don't, you will appear to be a phoney. Phoniness confuses people and acts as a turn-off. We crave honesty to such an extent that we'll often opt for the bare-faced rogue than do business with someone who appears to have something to hide.

So what can produce this incongruent image?

▶ You pick the wrong goals, aiming to be something that you are not and never will be, even with the wind working in your direction.

▶ You battle against your own visual and/or behavioural strengths, somehow seeing them as weaknesses.

What you should aim to do with your business body language is build on your strengths and delete any weaknesses. To do that you will need to understand a simple marketing strategy: always know the unique selling points (USPs) of the product you are trying to sell, in this case yourself.

So, what are your strengths? What are you good at? Why do people like you? List your positive qualities. Be objective about them. Why would you employ yourself? Why would you pick yourself as a friend?

What do you want to change? To change the image of something you need to address the following four things:

1. Product

Does this need any alteration before its relaunch? Will you need to do any work on inner confidence or self-esteem? Are you too negative? The greatest enemy you have when you tackle any self-improvement is yourself.

2. Process

How do you market yourself? Do you understand your successes and goals? Is your behaviour suitable to achieving those goals?

3. Positioning

Are you standing in the right spot right now? What is the market you are selling to? Who are your competitors? Are you tailoring your image to suit the right audience?

4. Packaging

How are you presenting yourself? How do others perceive that outer persona? Remember that misunderstanding your current and projected strengths and weaknesses will scupper any improvement plan.

USPs

Everyone has their unique selling points. Study any famous figures and you can work out what theirs were and what it was about their image that worked or not. Cometh the hour, cometh the man. Or woman. Or, at least, the image. Cultivating your own USPs will likewise achieve business and public 'buy in'.

It's not always as simple as it might seem, though. Honesty, you might assume, could only ever be considered a plus point, particularly in a political image. We all sleep better knowing the man or woman in charge is a person of integrity. So how should honesty look? It should mean dressing as you feel, rather than to please. And yet it was the 'honest' factor in Michael Foot's image – his wild flowing hair and casual dress – that did a lot of damage to his career as would-be UK Prime Minister. Apparently logical assumptions can go badly wrong especially when it comes to self-marketing.

Your level of ambition will also be an influence. The British, for example, love their eccentrics and parliamentary 'characters', like Dennis Skinner and the late Alan Clarke, but prefer to keep them out of reach of the very top spots. In business world-wide, the image of the company figurehead may be flamboyant, but only if it is in keeping with the image of the product. Bill Gates's 'computer nerd' image is as congruent to selling computers as Ben & Jerry's hippy look is to wild-flavoured ice cream. Anita Roddick suits 'natural' beauty products, while Versace's wealthy flamboyance was the ideal front for a fashion empire. Work out how high you are aiming and tailor your image goals accordingly. There is more on this in Chapter 5. For now, remember that the four best ways to scupper your own image success are:

1. Changing your image without being clear of your objectives.

2. Failing to recognise your USPs.

3. Assuming negative aspects of your character to be 'strengths'.

4. Modelling your behaviour on others' negative qualities, assuming them to be the root cause of their success.

Spin-cycle

Spin doctors are currently very fashionable, but they can be too prescriptive in their advice. Some apply the 'sheep-dip' approach, preaching 'smart, smug and slick' to everyone unlucky enough to pass through their hands. The whole point of bodytalk, though, is that there are very few 'rights' and 'wrongs'. Most success or failure is dependent on factors like timing, fashion preferences and trends, who appeared, spoke or did the job before, and a more intangible sense of charm, charisma or appeal. So, ignore image statistics or happy-clappy formulas for success. In fact, avoid all formulas like the plague.

When Richard Branson made a virtue out of a non-conformist image with his beard and pullover, lazier louts among the rest of us assumed that all they had to do was dress casual and stop shaving to make a mint overnight. And yet a heavy five o'clock shadow lost Nixon his first stab at the White House. Ken Livingstone snipped off the facial fuzz to become Mayor of London. Frank Dobson didn't. So does facial hair work or not? A beard is commonly seen as a non-business image and is generally frowned on in politics. But Branson has always set himself up as a bit of a buccaneer and his beard makes him look like Sir Walter Raleigh. So it fits. Never use simplistic evaluations.

Many men turn up on my courses wearing 'the statement tie', the statement usually being that they want to wear a likeness of Homer Simpson around their neck. Not funny and not clever, and I always make it my job to tell them so immediately, so we can get the stinging pain of personal taste insult over with and move on. Some, though, decide to fight their corner. 'Sir John Harvey-Jones wears lively neckwear' is a common response.

This is my reply and I want you to remember it: 'Sir John Harvey-Jones is an extremely clever and experienced business-man. His reputation arrives before the tie. He can wear more or less whatever he wants.'

The rest of us have to put in a bit of effort. We haven't got there yet.

▶ Current Image Plotting

So, where do we start from? When marketing companies start to work with a product they will often bullet-point words that relate to it. You can do the same. Make a list of all your personal quali-ties. Be objective. What do you do well? How do you come across? The list should be long.

Once you have trawled through your personality you will need to cast your eye over your current image reality. Stand in front of a full-length mirror, under good lighting. Close your eyes and rid your mind of all your personal subjective image perceptions. There are bits of your body you like and bits you hate. Some parts that you might even be obsessive over, like spots of cellulite or fat, maybe a pair of big feet or an over-generous nose. When you look at yourself in the mirror it is these bits you see, rather than the whole image. They become out of proportion, owing to your emotional input. What you are going to do now is to put them back into their place of rightful importance. Otherwise what you will be looking at is like a personally-sketched caricature, a visual exaggeration.

The next thing you will need to do while your eyes are shut is to get into a pose that will be familiar to other people. This is where you will have to rely on muscle memory to do the posing for you. When a mirror is around you will tend to pull yourself into some sort of shape you might like, rather than the one that will be familiar to colleagues at work. You are going to keep vanity well off the pitch at this point in the game.

Allow your face to drop into its habitual expression and ditto your posture. Do not try to please yourself, just go for what feels normal.

Open your eyes. And change nothing, even if your first reaction is one of unmitigated horror and depression bordering on the pathological.

Look at yourself without moving for a long, long time. Go on, keep looking. Flinch at nothing and ignore nothing.

If you look at your own reflection for long enough, you will get to the point where something strange happens. The person in the reflection is no longer the body your brain inhabits. You can look without prejudice. Try it, it works.

Once you have achieved this stage you are ready to take stock. Ask yourself the following questions:

1. Screen-saver

The 'screen-saver' expression is the one you wear in between your social, more contrived looks. Ask yourself:

▶ 'What does my face look like in repose? If my face were a T-shirt with a slogan on it, what would the slogan be saying? "Hello and welcome"? "I'm happy to be alive"? Or "Go away, I want to be alone"?'

▶ 'Do I look confident or do I wear the "hunted-and-haunted" look that is so popular in the business world? Would I trust myself if I saw myself gazing from the other side of a desk? Would I want to talk to myself at a party? Would I want to do business if I saw myself walking into my office?'

▶ 'Do my eyes show confidence, arrogance or passive acceptance? Do I look like a serial whinger? Is there a spark of passion or fun there? Or are they blank and mesmerised, like a rabbit caught in the headlights?'

2. Stance

Summarise the message from your posture. Do you stand tall and erect or are you sloping and stooped? If you were asked to pinpoint the energy focus of your body, where would you place it – around the head, shoulders, pelvis or feet? Does your body appear to sink into the ground like a puppet whose strings have been cut or does your vitality make you appear to 'float' from the shoulders and neck?

Looking for where your energy settles in your body is important when assessing your business image and impact. We'll be dealing with corrective work later on in the book, so your self-assessment at this stage is vital. Study the 'stance' drawings 1 to 4 (*overleaf*) and see which resembles your posture most closely.

3. Shoulders

Where do your shoulders lock when you are in repose? Do you tend to hold them high or pressed down quite low? Is there visible tension there or do they look loose and relaxed? How tightly are your upper arms held into your body? Do you tend to stand with your hands on your hips, freeing the upper arm completely? Look from the side. Are your shoulders straight, slumped or rounded? Look at the 'shoulders' drawings 1 to 4 (*see page 21*) and then check yourself in the mirror.

4. Feet

What shape do your feet take when you are static? Do the toes point inward or outward? How widely-spaced are your feet?

Stance

Slumped

Passive

Energetic

Arrogant

Shoulders

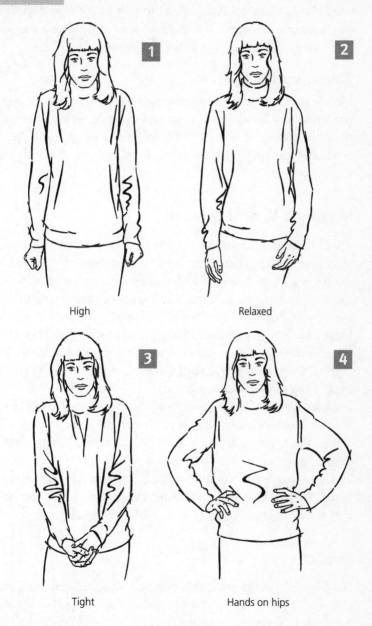

High

Relaxed

Tight

Hands on hips

Where do you move them to when altering your balance? If you need clarification, get hold of an old pair of shoes and study the way the heels are worn. The angle of wear should give you some clues. Do you stand on the outside or inside of your feet?

5. Arms and hands

Muscle memory tends to let us down badly when we try to park our arms in a familiar place, so just do what feels as normal as possible. Are your arms habitually folded or straight by your sides? Do you hold your hands together? If so, in what fashion do you clasp them?

Making a Map of Yourself

Try to draw an outline of what you see in the mirror. This will be your Image Map. There is no need to be artistic, all you are looking for is a 'map' of angles and shapes. Your mouth needn't look like your mouth, for example, but the overall arc should be right. While you are drawing, take note of statistics of body shape, too. How wide are your shoulders compared to your hips? How big is your head/torso/legs compared to the rest of your body? How high or long-waisted are you? How big do your hands and feet look? How long is your neck?

Make note of these proportions while your body is still in your 'muscle memory' pose. Don't stretch upright or iron out problem areas. What you are trying to map is your normal image, not the desired one.

There is no need to start being critical or analytical with your Image Map at this stage. Make no assumptions. Just remember that this map is a vital facet of your body language success.

Impact

Now I want you to grade this person you have been studying in terms of impact. Just go by looks for now and award points out of 10, with 0 being 'unmemorable' and 10 being 'noticeable and charismatic'.

If you voted on the side of 'noticeable', was it for positive or negative reasons? Was it for the intelligent-looking face or the baleful stare?

To help with this initial research you could enlist some help from a friend. What you need is some external assessment. Unadulterated, unbiased feedback is difficult to acquire, but what you can get are some snapshots of your screen-saver look. Get someone to take some pictures of you when you aren't posing. Forget the usual 'camera' smile, just stare right at the lens as though it were a stranger watching you silently. Do a couple of face shots, then some down to the waist and then a few full-lengths, including side and back views. When you get the results, pin them next to the map that you drew. This will be the current reality, that unmoulded plasticine that we'll be working on.

It doesn't matter if you don't like what you see, because you haven't started working with it yet. Bad can be good at this stage. Flawed current images are always the most fun because they offer the maximum opportunity for improvement. Just think, if you were an image consultant offering advice on smartening up, who would you most like to get your hands on to show off your talents, Alice Cooper or Mel Gibson? If you look in the mirror and see more of an Alice than a Mel staring back, then don't worry, the potential for improvement is overwhelming.

Endearing Habits?

When I said there are very few 'wrongs' in image construction I did not mean to say there are none at all. There are, of course, those bodytalk quirks that even the most dynamic spin doctor would be over-challenged to turn into a USP. These are the things you are least likely to know that you do. Or maybe you are aware of them and consider them to be amusing or even endearing. They will at best be annoying your colleagues and at worst disgusting them. And yet they are a common facet of all office life.

Avoid the following bodytalk – it will never create the winning touch:

▶ acts of self-grooming, i.e. nail, ear, tooth or nose-picking

▶ underwear-hiking

- ▶ knuckle-cracking

- ▶ crotch-fiddling

- ▶ sniffing

- ▶ nervous coughing

- ▶ persistent tapping or drumming

- ▶ semi-silent whistling

- ▶ jewellery-fiddling

- ▶ teeth sucking

- ▶ making air-quotes

- ▶ eating lunch in an open-mouthed feeding frenzy.

There are many more but I'm sure you can complete the list yourself.

▶ In Flagrante Delicto

The next stage of your self-assessment needs to involve more visuals, this time of you in action. You need as much video footage of yourself at work as possible. This visual view-fest is vital. You need to see yourself as others see you, warts and all.

Video footage is relatively easy to acquire. Most training courses provide it after role-play, or you could get a sympathetic colleague to film you while you work. Maybe you could get the firm's security guard to let you borrow some from the concealed cameras that seem to be an inevitability in most large companies these days.

When you watch yourself in action do the same trick as you did with your mirror image and pretend you are seeing someone you don't know. This should be easy, as we often fail to recognise our own CCTV image anyway, wondering who that po-faced person is in the monitored bank queue for a full three to four minutes before spotting the similarity to the face that stares at us out of the bathroom mirror each morning.

Study the image on screen several times (at least 10). Watch at least once without sound. Watch at least once with the sound turned up too loud. Watch at least three times on fast-forward to study patterns of movement. Watch without prejudice. Do not imagine corrections or fill up with emotional response. Do not look into the future, imagining how you can change. Judge only what you see on screen now. Then fill in the following questionnaire:

1. If you had seen this person giving a business presentation in your company how would you have assessed them (their status, depth of knowledge, personality etc)?

2. Did they seem to mean what they were saying, or were their gestures, tone and/or expression at odds with their words?

3. On a scale of 1 to 10, how would you rate their presence, charisma and impact?

4. How assertive did they appear to be?

5. Describe their posture.

6. Describe their hand gestures.

7. Describe their variety of facial expression.

8. Rate their level of eye contact.

9. Describe any other movement, like pacing or rocking.

10. Use three words to describe the person you watched.

What did you see that worked? What didn't work? What would be needed to get people to 'buy in' to the person you saw?

By now you should be ready to set some objectives. What are your visual objectives and what are the on-the-spot variables, by which I mean what margins of flexibility do you intend using at work?

'Rubber Masking': Situation Variables

Deciding on one set of image objectives can, of course, be dangerous. Different situations require different sets of tactics. So you need a degree of image flexibility when planning your bodytalk. You may decide to come across as an approachable little fun-bunny, but there may be clients who prefer the more formal approach. Perhaps you want to show authority in the office, but there may be times when you would prefer to be one of the crowd.

These chameleon tactics are appropriate in business. In fact you will find you are using them all the time, unless you are a 'take me as you find me' merchant, in which case you probably haven't even read this far.

Plan a broad canvas when creating the new you. Allow scope for any or all of the positives, while deleting any out-and-out negatives. Be prepared to study and tailor your style.

Key Points in a Nutshell

▸ Understand your USPs.

▸ Study yourself in the mirror and on video.

▸ See yourself from the outside in.

▸ Know your objectives.

▸ Be prepared to be flexible at work.

Chapter 2

Charisma and How to Get It

YOU MAY HAVE been hoping we'd start with a few small steps of self-improvement, like boosting your eye contact or showing you how to stop fiddling with your hands. But now is a good time to start on the overall picture and to begin targeting the bigger image goals, like charisma. 'Charisma' is a great word and a wonderful goal. Just thinking about being charismatic can make you begin to look and feel better.

Get back in front of that full-length mirror. Roll the word 'charisma' around on your tongue, then say out loud: 'I am charismatic. I look and feel great.' Your body should have started to respond already.

No? Well, I bet you stood up a bit straighter, at least.

▶ What is Charisma?

There are three strange and wonderful facts about charisma:

1. We'd all like to have it.

2. Most people think you have to be born with it.

3. When pressed, we don't really know what it is.

It's still a great word, though, and a fascinating concept.

To create charisma that consists of charm without smarm or arrogance you will need to feel good about yourself first. That's why this chapter will focus on techniques for enhanced self-esteem.

Pull out your Image Map and study your current reality again. How far is the person you see here from being charismatic?

Think back to your time at school. Every school, no matter how grim and ghastly, manages to turn out at least one charismatic pupil, someone who was universally admired and/or fancied, usually good at games and clever without being swotty. Little kids had crushes on them. Even the teachers liked them.

You may have started later in life, but it's never too late to start turning the charisma crank a few notches. It's not true to say you have to be born with charisma. It is usually something you start acquiring as you get older.

If you want a quick list of some of the qualities of a charismatic person, it would look a little like this:

- ▶ calm but energetic

- ▶ confident

- ▶ a good posture

- ▶ lively eyes and facial expression

- ▶ the ability to listen intensely.

Charismatic people can also be immensely beautiful, but immense beauty can just as easily accompany gormlessness.

People who have died usually find it easier to be charismatic than those still alive, because they're trading on reputation alone and are not up there queering their own pitch with non-charismatic lapses. We forget what they looked like in real life and see only the pictures and cinema footage. Stories are told that make them sound bigger. People start quoting them. John F. Kennedy, Marilyn Monroe, Greta Garbo, James Dean, Jackie Onassis, Che Guevara, Eva Peron – with all of these people the charisma may have been there in life but it's death that has sealed it in place as a non-negotiable quality.

▶ A Beginner's Guide to Charisma

Fortunately, you don't have to die to become charismatic. Think big, but begin with small, subtle stages of improvement:

1. Change the walk

Carry yourself tall. Walk smoothly and quickly. Hold your head up, instead of staring at the ground.

2. Travel light

Nothing you wear or carry should impede your posture or your gestures. Clutch at nothing and be weighed down by nothing. Royals always have some sort of presence and they rarely carry as much as a few quid in their pockets or bags, let alone a laptop, 12 Biros, a jar of hair gel, six old tissues and a pot of mango yoghurt.

3. Unravel your facial expression

Forget that dour, frowny screen-saver look which just sort of pops up when we're in between nicer expressions. Charismatic people never seem to wear a screen-saver expression, in fact I don't believe they even possess one. You needn't either. You can 'de-frown' your face with one easy exercise:

Exercise

Imagine a small iron is working its way around your facial muscles, smooth-ing them out. Stretch them a bit. Rearrange them into something altogether more pleasant and relaxed. Focus your mind on the word 'radiant'. Think of Nelson Mandela – his expression is one of almost permanent radiance.

The good thing about this is that it's also catching. People around you will start to unravel their faces as well. In fact, charismatic people nearly always get everyone smiling. You will never do that when you wear your screen-saver.

4. Stop moaning

Whingeing is to charisma what ice was to the *Titanic*. Whingeing doesn't just come out of your mouth, it seeps through every pore, expression and gesture. It is the biggest 'turn-off' in the history of communication. Charismatic people are entrancing conversationalists and moaning is not their style.

5. 'Aerobic listening'

Talking is not a prime requisite for the person with charisma. In fact many charismatic people of the past were either silent movie stars or people whose voices the public rarely heard. What many current charismatic people have, though, is the ability to listen well. They hone in on a person and make them feel special or important. So, show you are listening. Use eye contact, nodding and other visual responses to a person's points, and face-to-face and torso-facing posture.

6. Confidence

Charismatic people look comfortable in their own skin. They never come across as one of the 'walking wounded', those of us who carry ourselves in a way to imply we don't like being who we are or we disapprove of our own looks. Their confidence never spills over into arrogance. Shyness can work, though. Princess Diana managed to blend apparent shyness into the charismatic repertoire, while Hugh Grant excels at the diffidence routine.

Some people can even switch the charisma on and off. Actors can turn it on on stage and be insignificant off. Marilyn Monroe claimed she turned her charisma on with her special walk, that when she wasn't doing it people often ignored her in the street.

7. Integrity

Part of the charismatic portfolio is an inner integrity. Even when the quality is being switched on and off like a light bulb it still appears to be beaming out from inside, not painted on like cosmetics. That is what will build integrity and rapport.

This brings me back to the congruence factor. When your body language, words and tone of voice all dance in time people will usually believe the message. When these three are at odds with one another, apparent insincerity will raise its ugly head.

8. Self-rapport

So, you need to acquire 'self-rapport' if your communications are to work, especially when you are doing business masking. Customer care, in particular, will suffer if the 'Have a nice day!' looks and/or sounds phoney.

A psychologist called Mehrabian compiled a famous statistic on effective communication. He claimed that in terms of perceived impact of message in a face-to-face talk, the percentage break-down is: words 7 per cent; tone of voice 38 per cent; non-verbal signals 55 per cent.

Words are a low-impact factor because most people are poor 'ear listeners'. We allow boredom, short attention span, assumption or distractions to challenge our reception of the verbal message. Often we will interrupt or try to stack up responses or compete with the main message. When we have to listen for long periods of time, say to a speech or at a conference, our brains go off on loops, snatching a few words here and there and then sauntering off for a mental stroll around the block until we hear some more words that capture our attention.

Words supply a message but not necessarily its meaning. Try saying 'The building's on fire – run for your life' in a flat tone of voice and see who even stirs from their seat.

People also lie more easily with words, which is why we tend to distrust telephone communications more than face-to-face ones.

Vocal tone adds a further dimension. When you start to modulate your voice, adding pitch and variation, your listeners will begin to understand the meaning of what you have to say.

Non-verbal signals still make the lion's share of the impact, though. We remember what we see for longer than what we hear and we tend to rate visuals as a communication that is less easy to manipulate. This is another reason for making a study of your own visual messages.

▶ Leakage and How to Avoid It

I said that body language lying is possible, and it is. But, with time, the incongruent signals, like fiddling or foot-tapping, will give you away. These signals are called 'leakage' and it's easy to see why.

Try this experiment. Sit with someone who knows you well and tell them three stories about yourself, two genuine and one a blatant lie. Try to keep your body language signals, tone of voice and style of delivery the same throughout all three stories.

Even if you managed to avoid 'leaking' too much when you lied, you will have felt the extra – often massive – effort it takes to do so. The chances are that when you lied you 'over-responded', covering up the natural lack of eye contact with an unblinking stare and overacting the open, palm-up gesticulations. I expect you also became too wordy in your efforts to convince and that you started using terms like 'honestly', as well.

Leak-sealants

How can you avoid this kind of leakage? How can you appear confident when you are nervous or pretend to enjoy a job that is boring you to tears? How can you appear to like a client you detest or admire a boss you consider to be a prize idiot?

You have two choices:

1. Change your inner attitude.

2. Go to drama school.

I would suggest working on the internal feelings first.

You can start with a quick exercise to discover some patterns in your inner self-esteem. There is no score and no right or wrong answers, so be honest. The idea is to stimulate conclusions in your own mind.

Inner Esteem Self-Assessment

1. When you take your first look in the mirror in the morning, what thoughts go through your head?

2. How do you take a compliment?
   - ▶ I say, 'Thanks, that's great.'
   - ▶ I feel embarrassed.
   - ▶ Compliments? You must be kidding.
   - ▶ I wonder what the person's after.
   - ▶ I wonder whether they were really trying to tell me something was bad before.
3. Do you enjoy social occasions where you have to meet new people?
4. Do you enjoy going to social occasions alone and mingling?
5. Do you like working as part of a team or are you happier working alone?
6. Would you be daunted if you found yourself sharing a lift with your boss? (Or, if you are the boss, with one of your managers?)
7. Do you ever feel shy at work? If so, when?
8. If you were speaking to a new client for the first time, would you prefer to do it over the phone or face-to-face?
9. Do you tend to send e-mails when it would be just as easy to pop across and talk to the person?
10. Do you enjoy chatting at work and have a bit of a reputation for it?
11. What kind of business communications do you find the most difficult and why?
12. Do you enjoy going on a visit to a new company or does the thought make you nervous?
13. If you were called in to see the boss today, would you expect it to be good or bad news?
14. How good do you think you are at inter-personal communications, like staff appraisals or team briefings?
15. Do you plan key business communications beforehand or just go with the flow?
16. Do you think other members of staff like you?
17. If you spot two colleagues whispering about you, do you assume they are being positive or critical? If critical, what do you think they are being critical about?
18. Which work situations make you the most nervous?
19. Analyse why this is. Make a list of the reasons.
20. As you stand up to start a business presentation, what do you think is going through the heads of your audience?
21. Would you mind walking the full length of an open-plan office, knowing people were watching you?

22. Do you enjoy new challenges at work or prefer sticking to routine tasks?
23. Do you seek praise from others to make yourself feel more confident about your work skills or do you tend to praise yourself?
24. How often do you criticise yourself, your work or the way you look to colleagues?
25. Are you good at speaking up at meetings?
26. If you deal with a customer face-to-face, do you find yourself taking things personally and responding emotionally if they have a complaint?
27. Do you ever use phrases like: 'I know this might sound stupid ...' before you raise a point at work?
28. Do you enjoy selling or find it embarrassing?
29. Do you find you tend to be passive at work, agreeing to take on too much in the spirit of 'anything for a quiet life'?
30. Write down 20 reasons why you are a valuable asset for your company.

▶ Love Me, Love My Boss

Learning to love your boss/colleagues/clients may not always be an option. Building inner confidence and self-esteem is, though. And when your self-confidence starts to grow, your response to negative stimuli – like ratty bosses and moody colleagues – becomes easier to change.

You may not be able to change other people's behaviour or certain circumstances of your job, but you should always retain control over the response they provoke in you. Never allow yourself to be contaminated by other people's bad moods or behaviour. *You* decide how you want to think and act, not other people. Rudeness, moodiness and stress do not have to be absorbed. You can choose not to be affected by them.

Build your self-confidence by analysing the situations that cause it to drain. Perhaps it's when you meet people for the first time, are called in to see the boss, are dealing with a difficult customer, have to make small-talk at a business function or give a major presentation in front of a large audience. Any or all of these situations may provoke panic. So you may avoid them. But that simply means that with time, you get worse at them, rather than better.

The sequence tends to run as follows:

Stimulus: 'I have a keynote presentation to make next week.'

Negative response: 'I'm a terrible presenter.'

Emotive response: 'I feel nervous and anxious.'

Negative affirmation: 'I know I will screw up.'

To break the run of negative thinking that becomes a self-fulfilling prophesy you need to break the line of inner communication:

▶ Stop after the first statement, which is the only one that needs to be factual: 'I have a keynote presentation to make next week.'

▶ Throw in a positive affirmation at this point, even if you don't believe the statement to be true: 'I'm a good presenter. I'm looking forward to the event.'

▶ Keep repeating this phrase in your head to block out the process that leads to negative emotional responses.

▶ Expect your negative inner dialogue voice to keep scoffing and denying the positive affirmation, but ignore it. You know it won't help on the day.

The other action step is to keep doing whatever it is you are worried about. Do as many presentations as possible. Chair the meetings. Go to all the functions. It is the only way to rehearse. Avoidance will only make things worse. Stretch yourself way outside your comfort zone. Do so regularly. If you keep moving in this direction, the chances are you'll move through discomfort to a new learned skill.

Talk yourself to confidence. Tell yourself you are good and visualise yourself doing well. Approach each situation with enthusiasm, not dread. Coach your own mind towards positive responses. Charisma doesn't sit well with paranoia, so you need to learn to become what is called a 'reverse paranoid'. Expect people to like you. Assume they are thinking the best of you. If they act coldly when you approach them, tell yourself they are only lacking in confidence, just as you used to be. If you see yourself being discussed out of earshot, imagine the comments are favourable, rather than scathing. Tell yourself that people want to listen when you speak, that if they ignore you it's only because they didn't hear you. Never allow yourself to feel unimportant because that can never be true, even if you only have a fan-base of one – yourself.

Self-affection

You should like yourself very much. If you don't, then change your behaviour to become a person you do like. Very few patterns of behaviour are unchangeable. Just because you were shy, nervous, pessimistic, spineless, lazy and untidy yesterday and every day before that, it doesn't mean that you have to be the same tomorrow and all the following days. It's never too late to reinvent yourself. And it can be fun!

Throw in a few changes just for change's sake, just to prove you can shuck off old patterns. Paint your toenails. Iron your socks. Find a couple of good jokes and learn to tell them well. Then you can graduate to the big stuff, like changing patterns of diffidence and anxiety into confidence. To do this you will need a specific work plan.

Exercise

Building on ideas gathered in the first exercise *(see pages 32–4)*, mark out three columns on a piece of paper to list all the situations at work that make you feel uncomfortable, shy or lacking in confidence.

Beside each situation, in the second column, write a description of how you would *like* to feel, look and act during those situations.

Use the third column to list all the actions you will take to work towards feeling, looking and acting in the style you prefer.

For example:

Column one: At noisy meetings I feel awkward, embarrassed, afraid of speaking up, worried that my point isn't worth making.

Column two: I would like to speak in a way that commands attention, to speak clearly, in a concise, confident manner. I would like to be looking around the room, smiling and using open gestures to add emphasis to what I am saying.

Column three: I will:
- ▶ study the agenda and plan my key points before the meeting
- ▶ rehearse positive body language
- ▶ use inner self-coaching messages to improve my confidence
- ▶ listen actively to other speakers to ensure my points are valid
- ▶ learn to get rid of waffle and negative speech patterns.

This turns a wish-list into a comprehensive work plan, one that you intend using.

You may never rid yourself of *all* your shyness, nerves or lack of confidence, but I don't believe you need to try. Some of these feelings may help to improve your performance. They give us the buzz that makes us powerful and active. But they should never stand in the way of what we want to achieve. Sort out the stuff that prevents you from getting up there and giving your best.

▶ Stress Response

Stress is very much part of that stuff. Few jobs come without their own raised stress levels. Some companies even boast about the stressfulness of their jobs and the suffering is seen as part of the challenge.

Stress affects us in three ways. It affects our intellect, our physical health and our emotions. When you work with manageable stress levels, you think more quickly and clearly. When you teeter into 'over-stress', your thinking goes into survival mode, which cuts off all your higher intellect, recalled memory and creative and intuitive faculties.

Healthwise, you start to suffer from a whole raft of problems, including headaches, muscle tension, indigestion, palpitations, backache and sleeplessness.

Emotionally, you can become like a wilful five-year-old. Again, the survival response kicks in, causing exaggerated emotional displays. You can get picky, snappy, tearful or angry for little or no cause. You stop playing team games because paranoia kicks in and you no longer want to share your toys. You take everything personally, from customer complaints to the way that the lift always takes a long time to come.

Stress can be visible, too. Imagine the stress response in terms of body language. Different people will have different symptoms, but they can all lead an observer to the conclusion that they are overdoing things.

Stress Bodytalk

▶ Muscle tension increases, often leading to raised shoulders.

▶ The blink rate can increase.

▶ Movements become less co-ordinated. We become jerky or clumsy.

▶ Gestures and expressions can become as spontaneous as our speech patterns.

▶ Body language 'leakage' increases. The smaller gestures betray tension, like hands forming into fists or excessive tapping or fiddling.

▶ Tensions will be displayed in the facial expression. Eyes widen, eyebrows are raised.

If the stress levels become severe, depression can result. This will lead to less physical activity as the adrenaline fails to hit and tiredness steps in. Shoulders may slump at this stage, body movements lessen and facial expression revert to a frown or spasm of anxiety.

Verbally, you can tell everyone at work that you are OK, but your body signals may warn them that all is not well, even if they may only read these signals on a subliminal level and then not know why they think something is up.

But when we are stressed at work it is ourselves we tend to lie to the most. We say we are busy but coping, or that we thrive under pressure. We become the office martyr, refusing to delegate or turn work down. This denial emerges – like other factors – as visual incongruence. We look stressed and tired, but we are agreeing to accept more work. We use the phrase 'no problem' frequently, when anyone with half an eye can see that it is. Again, this incongruence in communicated signals leads to distrust. And as the emotions become more acute, so do the displays of irritation or upset, however much we may try to mask them.

Creating Calm

So, quite simply, stress will not enhance your bodytalk. Your movements will lack fluidity, your expression will tighten, gestures become erratic and muscle tension show throughout your posture, particularly in the shoulders. The picture is not a pretty one. You are in survival mode and colleagues will sense the underlying aggression in your aura. By trying to act relaxed you will only take on the appearance of a 'stress martyr', which will make other people uncomfortable to be around you. Tension is airborne and others will catch it. Hence the office that becomes like a startled flock where only one sheep saw the danger and the others panicked blindly.

There should now be a long list of tips to 'de-stress', but there isn't. Stress is not a 'one size fits all' problem. Different things stress out different people. A cure for one will be what can tilt another over the brink. I was never so stressed as when I sat in a yoga class, yet for most people it is the ultimate salvation. Personally, I de-stress on Heavy Metal, which could turn you feral.

To gain greater awareness of your own stress patterns, take some time to answer the following questions. They are simple in concept yet may provide the key to your de-stress work.

1. What levels of stress do I work best at?

2. How long can I sustain that level of pressure, challenge and effort before I need to take time out?

3. What are the symptoms that tell me I need a break because I am overdoing it?

4. What are the large problems that I find difficult to manage at work?

5. What are the smaller matters like petty annoyances that drive me into over-stress?

6. What do I think are the three key external factors that cause my over-stress, like lack of time, impossible deadlines, office politics, impossible manager, etc?

7. How and when do I find it easiest to relax and create calm?

8. What is the balance between work stress and home stress?

9. Do I take work stress home and home stress to work?

10. Considering the fact that stress can be a killer, are the problems and situations that stress me out really worth dying for?

Working on the symptoms of stress will not be enough, you also need to challenge your mental perceptions. Work is rarely a matter of life or death, but we respond almost as though it is. Do whatever you can to get things into context. The people I meet who have the healthiest attitude to their jobs are often the ones who have had a clear warning. Perhaps they have had a heart attack. Perhaps a child or partner has been through a major health scare. Some serious problem has forced them to change their perspective on life. They now know what matters and what doesn't. The trivia of work no longer affects them. They are professional but relaxed.

Don't wait for a disaster before you achieve that level of philosophical thought. Work on your attitude first. And remember that charisma!

Key Points in a Nutshell

▶ Build congruence in your image.

▶ Be wary of your screen-saver face.

▸ Understand how 'leakage' can work and what your own signals tend to be.

▸ Seal off the leaks by working on inner feelings and self-esteem. Use positive inner dialogues and self-coaching to build confidence.

▸ 'Grow' your confidence in specific situations by stretching yourself on a daily basis.

▸ Write out a work plan to deal with any situations you see as 'tricky'. Plot feelings and align them with actions. Study the problems and start to overcome them.

▸ Work on keeping your stress levels manageable.

Chapter 3

Down to Business

ONCE YOU HAVE set your image targets you need to be clear of your career goals. How high do you want to fly? Which particular job do you have your eye on, or do you intend your success to involve being in charge of your own company?

And before you start being modest, can I just add two words: Stuff modesty.

Modesty is dishonesty when it's part of your inner dialogue. There's no need to brag to outsiders, but inside you can be bold in your plans. Think as big as you like and bigger.

So, what do you want to achieve? How should you sell yourself? What will be your target audience? Whom will you need to communicate successfully with? Whom do you need to persuade and influence? The success or failure of any communication depends on how it is honed for the listener. Will all of your key players appreciate the same 'you' or will you need to build a variable image profile?

▶ Build Your Own Marketing Profile

Plan 'product objectives'. Look at the four-box option:

1. Existing product to existing clients

This is the no-risk, no-gamble box. You carry on looking as you have always looked and dealing with the people you have always dealt with. If you always do what you have always done, you will always get what you always got. It's up to you to decide whether this is enough or whether you want to aim higher.

2. Existing product, new clients

You put yourself about a bit more, but without changing first. You network and raise your profile. Without checking your image-fitness, though, this can be counter-productive. Before you raise your profile you should work on enhancing it.

3. New product, existing clients

You improve your image, then sell it to existing clients. This is useful if the product is something other than yourself, but limited otherwise, unless you feel the need to reinvent yourself. When an existing image has become stereotyped negatively, however, this can be extremely effective.

4. New product, new clients

The biggest gamble in some ways, but offering the greatest pay-off. You work on your image and then set about marketing it by raising your profile.

Dress to Suit

As an example of variable image behaviour to new and existing clients, take the big financial companies in the UK, many of whom have recently opted to switch to 'down-dressing', i.e. smart/casual wear, instead of the traditional formal suits. This change has been radical in terms of culture and perception. It was also very much an elected change, rather than an organic one. Some companies had evolved to the stage of a one-day dress-down policy, but others went from city slickers to urban warriors or sports slacks overnight.

A couple of the larger firms unveiled their new look in the press, receiving massive exposure. Your own image change will be more gradual, on a smaller scale, and probably much less news-worthy. However, there are parallels in terms of the potential success or failure of the project.

One of the first fascinating factors is what were the companies trying to achieve? If you look at their philosophy, you can compare your own in terms of variables. The reasons given were roughly as follows:

1. The staff like the look.

2. It will increase performance.

3. It will keep us in line with the rest of the world, which tends to down-dress for business.

4. It will remove barriers when dealing with clients.

5. It will project an image of change, innovation and modernity to our clients.

6. The MD likes wearing slacks.

7. Shares in companies abroad rose when similar schemes were introduced.

Now, any or all of these can be a sound objective. If you are unclear about your final goal, though, your changes will come unstuck. This is currently the case with the down-dressing. The jury is still out on the 'staff will like it' idea. Some do and some don't. Some find it stressful, as they no longer know what is 'appropriate'. Some staff disapprove of the casual-wear style of others. As a 'personnel puff' there were probably better schemes to consider, including a pay rise.

As for impressing the customer, companies needed to be sure exactly *how* they intended to impress. If it was by changing the signature look of the company to something more relaxed and trendy, then that needed to be the new look whatever the circumstances. Some companies are still undecided, though, telling staff to dress up when visiting more formal companies.

If the aim was to keep the MD happy, or cause a hike in shares and that is what has occurred, then perhaps the objective has been met.

Such 'image decisions' are not only made by companies, of course. Rock stars have similar decisions to make. Their desired projected image needs to be defined early on in their career if they are going to appeal to their target audience. Are they going for the younger pop market or do they want to attract an older following? Should they be clean-cut or will the bad boy image sell better? Often there will be little or no flexibility of goals. Alienation of non-target audience is as much a USP for performers as attracting the desired crowd.

The important factor with your own image is to think any changes through in advance. Keep the end result in mind. Target the right audience. Your success will depend on it. Do you want your new overall image to impress bosses, colleagues, clients, shareholders and/or public opinion or just yourself? Do you want to merge into the current corporate identity or spark off on a lone success trail? Do you want to be famous? Do you want to be low or high-profile? Paul Getty or Richard Branson?

Some of these decisions will be taken on the hoof, as image needs to be flexible on a working level, as well as focused on the core goals. Perhaps you can create messages that will appeal to everyone. Or perhaps you will have to duck and dive on a daily basis, creating a different set of personas for each meeting or communication. This may sound like abject insincerity, but it needn't be. Adaptability is a core value in the skill of communication and rapport. It will enhance your skills of persuading, influencing and negotiating.

A Passion for Fashion

Fashion will, of course, influence your image, however much you may resist it. We are all slaves to fashion to some degree. Some of the most fun and the worst bodytalk disasters have been the result of techniques we have picked up as fashion items.

Clothing fashion has been a great influence on bodytalk, especially for women. Heels have varied in height over the past six decades from six-inch stilettos to backward-leaning eco-sandals, and every heel change will affect the way we move. Pencil skirts in the Fifties introduced a virtual hobble and meant getting on and off buses sideways-on. Minis in the Sixties led to the Quant-style knees-together-ankles-wide-apart way of sitting to avoid showing off knickers. Trousers and 'comfy' shoes as workwear in the Eighties and Nineties meant more freedom of movement for women and standing and sitting postures that began to ape the men. Current fashions are moving back to pencil skirts and kitten heels, so tottering is once more the order of the day.

There seems to be no evolution with this fashion factor. Liberation is won and lost and most of it is entirely meaningless. Bras that were burnt in the Seventies came back as upholstered as ever in the Nineties. Vivienne Westwood went from introducing liberating aggressive-girl punk to bringing back bustles and crippling platforms that even pushed Naomi Campbell to her limit on the catwalk.

What can change for both sexes is the body fashion image. Women in the Sixties and Seventies were expected to look doe-like and vacant. You didn't have to smile or show energy or life in the eyes, in fact corpse-like was the norm. Biba girls were hugely expressionless. Twiggy and Penelope Tree specialised in the beautifully gormless gaze. Men suffered a similar fate, with Bowie and Bolan as posturing vacuous-looking role-models.

Then it all turned sexy in the late Seventies, with more of a Pan's People/Barbie/beauty queen image with big eyes and a permanent smile of ecstatic delight. Women were expected to pout and play dumb. TV hostesses did little more than fake orgasms over fridges and coffee pots and women in support roles at work were expected to do the same, while men either got laddish and dressed like the Sweeney, or foppish, like Jason King.

The Eighties started the shift towards corporate culture and women were expected to look bright for the first time. Hair went like fright wigs and power-dressing was the norm. Prior to the stock market crash the Yuppies ruled and body language between the sexes became similar as we all thought the Porsche and multi-million bank balance was within our grasp. Women still smiled more than men but were also allowed to look troubled, because therapy was all the rage.

Today the unisex look is still a feature, but not uniformly so. Down-dressing has seen a further layer of de-sexing as both men and women turn up in the office clad in combats and T-shirts. Fashion is still changing, though. Women are currently re-embracing Seventies structured workwear while men are clinging to chinos and deck shoes.

Role-models

Body language itself has never been so popular as a fashion item as it is now. TV and film stars have become icons as much for the way they move or the facial expressions they use as the way they dress – perhaps even more so in some cases. Julia Roberts and Tom Cruise do it with a smile, while Schwarzenegger has his trademark scowl.

The stars of cult programmes like *Friends* and *Buffy the Vampire Slayer* have mined a rich seam in innovative body fashions. People flap like Phoebe and copy the slow-react eye-roll of Ross just as much as they mimic the odd verbal emphasis of Chandler. Ditto with the *Buffy* cast. Few people can smoulder like Angel, but anyone can copy Willow's hand-waving, facially-meandering kookiness.

Teenagers use 'fusion' gestures, creating a blend of gestures, expressions and movement from different cultures. The comedian Sacha Baron-Cohen used this fusion style between black and white to make his name as Ali G, complete with high fives and rapper gestures.

Another fascinating current trend is for the 'virtual gesture'. This is where the person acts out their retrospective feelings or emotions, almost in the third person. The words run something like: 'Carl told me yesterday that the project had been cancelled and I was like: "Wow! Hey! Oh my God!'" This will be accompanied by acted response (often over-acted). The effect is one of clinical detachment. You might not find this suitable for your business image, though.

Body Language Jargon

Business tends to throw up its own gesture jargon, which likewise goes in and out of fashion. Like verbal jargon, this takes the form of a 'gesture pool' that tends to get shared by everyone in the company. Copying gestures or expressions from higher up the status ladder provides workers with the comforting notion that these are the correct ones to use. Some of them are strictly corporate and do not see light of day outside the workplace.

I recently witnessed an amazing office community gesture of tie-flicking. There were at least 50 men in this open-plan office and each one flicked his tie over his shoulder the minute he straightened up from the desk.

'Fashion' bodytalk can be fun, but remember to move on quickly or you can look stale.

▶ Action and Reaction

Unlike fashion, many psychologists believe our personalities to be virtually unalterable, except by traumatic events or changes in our lives. Changing your image is a different matter, though. Your behaviour is always variable. You can always change what you do, even if you have little control over who you are.

In work it is vital we take control over our own behaviour and responses. Reacting, rather than responding, to situations can be catastrophic to your career. Reaction is the immediate behaviour, fuelled by emotion, rather than logic. In terms of business results it is usually the wrong call.

What happens is that the emotional brain will pull out what is perceived as the 'natural' reaction – something impulsive and focused on self-centred feelings. The thinking brain will tend to pause, plan and respond. It works on learned responses that are rational and based on mutual gain. It tends to look at the bigger picture, focusing on overall objectives, rather than the knee-jerk stuff the emotional brain serves up.

As an example, imagine a colleague has corrected your point in the middle of a presentation to the MD of a client company. You know the point you made was right. Your emotional brain will tell you to stand up for yourself and prove your colleague wrong in front of the MD. Perhaps you will want them to be as humiliated as you just felt when they corrected you. Perhaps you want to vent your anger. Reacting like this will improve the situation in one way only: it will make you feel better. But possibly only for a short while. In the meantime you could have dented the reputation of your entire company by getting into public conflict with your colleague. The MD will probably see both of you in a bad light.

The thinking brain would have told you to hold fire. It would have stayed fixed to the main objective of the meeting, which was to impress the client and make the sale. This controlled response would have led you to a different style of behaviour. You would have thanked your colleague for the correction and carried on in a calm manner. This would have created a more effective image and been in line with your overall goals.

That said, you *are* allowed to have emotions in business. After all, you are human. Emotions can be useful, but they should never scupper your main objective. You still need to make decisions about when to mask them.

Look at people who have included an emotional display in their image repertoire. Some worked and some didn't. Paul Gascoigne's tears in the World Cup sealed his fame as a sporting personality and endeared him to his audience. Job-wise, it was flawed, though. Watch the captain Gary Lineker during the same piece of film footage. He appears to be warning the manager to keep an eye on Gascoigne. He was upset and his game could have suffered.

Margaret Thatcher's tears at being moved out of office stemmed from entirely different emotions and brought a different set of responses from her audience. The sadness was prompted mainly by self-loss and there was a sense of shock at seeing someone apparently invincible being reduced to tears.

In business people expect professional control and so will remember the time that you lost it, even momentarily. Emotional displays are also very visual and people remember visual images long after words or even deeds are forgotten. Do you want to be remembered as the person who lost their temper or burst into floods of tears? A better idea would be to have the right image for your career goals.

▶ Evolution

You can compare human bodytalk to that of animals in many basic functions. Even the 'sophisticated' business person is still sometimes governed by animal responses. Understanding how some of your baser instincts affect you at work will lead to greater success as you are able to challenge your emotional or knee-jerk responses and substitute logical, more effective behaviour.

Evolution in body language responses has been vital to survival in the modern business world. In an overcrowded arena we have had to learn to cope with the 'comfort' of strangers and in many ways we have been forced to overrule our evolutionary instincts.

Personal Boundaries

One of the defining needs of human mental well-being is for space and territorial ownership. Animals will fight to the death over terrain. Wars are caused by it. Punch-ups break out in pubs because of it. We have very precise cultural and evolutionary rules about how close people can get to us. The theme of spatial awareness will be a recurring one in this book because it affects our business lives enormously.

You have three sets of boundaries around you that you wear like invisible hoops. The closest area to your body is called the intimate zone. The distance from body to boundary will vary according to upbringing and cultural variations. In the UK the intimate zone usually extends about 18 inches from the body. In most other countries it does not extend so far. This is the space reserved for people whom you are comfortable being touched by. Without extensive knowledge of your personal habits I would hazard a guess that this does not include many people.

The next zone is known as the social zone and is the space reserved for people who are known to you. They don't have to be friends but they do need to be people you either know or have assumed knowledge of. At a business function, for instance, everyone will space themselves according to social zone requirements.

Strangers live beyond this area. If a stranger invades the social zone we become twitchy. We become more observant, aware that protocol has been breached. If the stranger goes on to invade the intimate zone, we are on full alert, the body tensed for fight or flight. The stranger in the intimate zone will either be unaware of the evolutionary ground rules of engagement (i.e. stupid, and therefore a potential nuisance) or flaunting them deliberately (i.e. physically threatening or sexually predatory). On a bad day we may be dealing with an idiotic pervert.

There are situations, of course, like commuting, which breach this code of spatial behaviour on a regular basis. The normal conditions of rush-hour commuting would be untenable if humans had not evolved to be able to cope. In our raw animal state we would probably suffer from stress to the point of breakdown. Underground travel, in particular, would be more than enough to trigger the madness switch. You are crammed into a metal tube beneath the earth with hundreds of strangers, many of whom are close enough to be touching you. While enjoyable enough for your average run-of-the-mill *frotteur*, for most 'normal' people this crush would be unbearable.

So we need to apply rules of safety and normality. We need an 'I am crushing you, but I am no threat' body language signal. The result has been the 'no eye contact' pose. When strangers are legitimately forced into intimate spatial distances any eye contact will be accidental and fleeting. In a crowded lift we look at the floor-numbers panel or stare at the floor. On the underground we will read a newspaper, study the mindless ads or stare dumbly into space.

While occupied like this, though, at the same time we will be on the look-out for potential threats. These may be obvious, like the flasher or the gang of noisy hooligans, or subtle, say a strange person using eye contact or smiling at other passengers. Again, we will see these strangers as people who either do not understand the rules or who have chosen to deliberately flout them.

Our inner awareness of these unwritten 'space laws' is strong. We understand the rules of engagement and will usually toe the line without murmur. We know on an instinctual level how important they are.

Marking Your Territory

We only have to settle into a space for a short amount of time before we consider it to be 'ours' and we may mark it as our territory. If you leave a jacket on a chair in a pub, for example, no matter how crowded the place gets, everyone will obey the rules and leave the seat alone. If the jacket is moved, it will be seen as an overt act of aggression. The same applies to towels on sun-loungers. Seeing them makes holiday-makers angry, but actively moving them signals open warfare.

In most jobs territorial marking is not a problem, but the animal instinct is strong. If you want to unsettle a colleague, get into work before them and let them arrive to find you sitting at their desk. Be polite. Ask if they mind and explain you had to do this for a reason. They will probably insist it's OK, but watch their body language 'leakage'. On an animal level they will be horribly disturbed to have found another creature in their nest.

Hot-desk Survival

Not surprisingly, the modern trend for 'hot-desking', where no one desk is reserved for no one employee's usage, has had a permanent unsettling effect on employees. Desks in this culture are usually shared out on a first-come first-served basis. All personal equipment has to be cleared away each night and often placed in a locker. But people expect spatial ownership and like to mark their territory, which is why they tend to display so many toys and personal touches around their workstation. Depriving people of this basic need could cause massive stress. So hot-deskers have needed to evolve.

Pushing people out of their worknests can have two outcomes: either they will start to nest ferociously outside the workplace or they will become totally nomadic. Crowded cities mean the ferocious nesting option is often untenable. Your parents and grandparents would probably have had the luxury of their 'own' seat on the bus or train and in the pub in the evening. If they dined regularly in a restaurant they would have been offered their 'usual' table. If the living space was small they might have used a potting shed or allotment or a study as their nest at home. Cultures change, though. You are probably lucky if you have created the habit of your own seat in your own house to use every evening. And yet once each armchair would have been sacrosanct territory in a living room.

City-dwelling business people have turned into nomads, then, eating out in different restaurants, socialising in a variety of bars, even partnering more people and walking away from relationships with greater ease. Territorial markings have become less structured and yet they can remain firmly ensconced in many surprising areas of work life.

Petty Conflicts

If you have ever moved to new premises you will know about all the internecine warfare that breaks out over territory and space. Complex issues are involved here. Apart from being possessive about any terrain we deem to be our own, we also see a connection between space and status. If you are moved from your office into a smaller one, the move will be seen as a job downgrade, no matter how much evidence to the contrary. And I'm not just talking about large changes. Desk and chair size is part of the same issue. Big office, big desk, big chair, big boss. Also, big paranoia if that rule is abused. You may try to pretend it doesn't matter, but it does.

Ownership of territory can be achieved in a matter of seconds. Go on a training course and you will either be given a seat in the room or asked to choose your own. Either way that chair and whatever desk goes with it will become yours and yours alone for the duration of the course. The quickest way to upset delegates is to change their name cards around overnight. They will always arrive on day two expecting to sit in the same chair as they did on day one. The need is a great one, even if they are not aware of it until they notice that they are to sit somewhere different. A seat only needs to be ours for a few moments before it has turned into a nest in our minds. Beneath the surface we are still territorial animals.

Fast-track Friends and New Packs

Work has also taught us how to evolve in terms of stranger-touch and fast-track stranger-bonding, as with a new client whom we have to treat as a friend without knowing whether they pose a threat or not. Most animals will display aggression until the 'stranger' animal has proved friendly. Humans in business have to display the opposite. So we cope with these situations by masking.

Many customer care courses follow the 'heavy on the eye contact, big on the grin' philosophy of client-pleasing, yet both those signals are an abuse of first-meeting rules outside the workplace. Heavy-duty eye contact is reserved for lust, love or fight signalling in the real world, and yet any trip to the counter of a burger bar can result in your being on the receiving end of an intense stare. Really broad smiles should signal an advanced stage of hysteria or pleasure, and yet they are regularly flashed as a greeting at clients before anyone has even spoken.

Touch is an equal intimacy, yet we are expected to use it to break down barriers in first-stage business greetings. Rules need to apply to avoid charges of sexual misconduct and so the business handshake was invented.

We have also had to learn to lose the old taboos about eating. Food can be consumed anywhere in the modern workplace, from the desk where you sit to the stairwell, lift or even street as you walk along. This latter non-safe eating environment is an abuse of the basic animal need to consume in a corner.

We have had to evolve in order to cope with changing pack behaviour as well. In business, packs, i.e. teams, are formed and disbanded almost overnight. Rivalry is often encouraged between departments, but then the edict goes round that the whole company should work as one team. Pack leaders, i.e. managers, come and go and, during mergers, a takeover from a rival company can often mean staff have to see old adversaries as part of their new team.

And yet we evolve to cope with all this, no matter how much it flies in the face of nature and social law. Somehow we learn to handle it and often we end up almost enjoying it. We still need to be aware of the animal that lurks inside the city slicker, though. It is never completely tamed. So bear this in mind as you get to work on developing your new business bodytalk.

Key Points in a Nutshell

▶ Know your business goals.

▶ Position yourself in the marketplace – do you have the right image?

▶ Understand fashion trends and how they affect perception.

▶ Work on your emotions. Study them objectively. Start to learn to mask them, if necessary.

▶ Understand the way you use space in relation to others around you.

Chapter 4

*B*odytalk Skills

Now you have your big picture goals in place, it's time to look at your body language in more detail. Your body language signals can be divided into six groups:

1. Long-range signalling

This includes your posture and the way you propel your body. You have 'signature' ways of walking, sitting and standing. A partner could recognise you at a distance from these movements alone. They will be affected by mood, stress and health.

2. Limb language

The arms and the legs tend to 'conduct' as we speak. When we are orally silent the signals still keep flying.

3. Micro-movement

These are the smaller gestures, like hand, finger or foot movements, that provide a constant insight into your thoughts. Some of these movements are so speedy and small that they are almost invisible to the naked eye.

4. Face behaviour

The eyes are the most potent and subtle signallers in our repertoire.

Beneath the skin of the face, though, lie a myriad of muscles which are able to perform complex gyrations. Unlike the body posture, even minute alterations in the facial landscape can signal immense changes of mood and thought.

5. Spatial behaviour

All animals are affected by space and proximity. Comfort, safety and perceptual well-being can all be devastated by inappropriate spatial behaviour, or, to put it bluntly, standing too close can give people the creeps.

6. Touch

Touching other people in business produces high-impact results. Need I add more at this point?

All these skills will add up to create the cluster signals that form your own non-verbal communications. Some are more powerful than others. Touch and space are often the dominant communicators, although message transmission will depend on overall balance.

Bodytalk needs to also cover smell and grooming. Whether these come under the long-distance signals or the more subtle kind in your case, only you and your friends, colleagues and dog will know. I also like to include business dress even though it is body adornment, rather than movement. You will be aware by now that business dress is an important part of your image, signalling tribal or pack awareness, inner perceptions, mood, self-belief and status.

Never get over-excited by only one facet of your bodytalk skills. You need to be aware of the overall balance in order to present yourself well. A good smile can be a great way to welcome a customer, but it will be negated if you have neglected to work on your hand messages and eye contact. I have coached businesspeople into greeting with a lovely smile, only to see it paired with staring, aggressive eye contact or a handshake that could crack walnuts.

Where the Heck ...?

It may interest you to know where you got your own particular set of bodytalk variances from. It would be great to make a specific list, but mind-science is rarely that precise. A rough guide to the various sources would go something like this, though:

1. Inborn responses

These will be the gestures and movements that you would have used even if you'd been brought up by sperm whales or spent your formative years wandering alone in the woods. As there are rarely cases of either occurrence, however, it's hard to truly know which movements are inborn and which are learned. Smiling to show pleasure and shaking the head from side to side to refuse unwanted food seem to be the sort of things we would do anyway.

A lot of other emotional displays have survival as their core purpose. When we register surprise, for instance, the eyes widen and the brows raise. This will enhance our vision in an attack or danger situation.

2. Plagiarism

These are the expressions and gestures we pick up through copying another person. They amount to by far the greater percentage. Children learn by copying adults and as adults we're still at it to a greater or lesser degree. Staff might mimic a boss they admire or fear, or whose job they covet.

In business we use the technique of 'modelling', especially when we start a new job and particularly if that job has a strong cultural initiative. We may be doing this consciously or, like taking on an accent when we spend time in a distant place, we may not be aware we're doing it until someone from outside the workplace comments on it. This forms part of the process often known as 'corporate cloning'.

3. Involuntary plagiarism

This is the stuff of nightmares. It's when you pick up bodytalk 'habits' and routines that you *don't* want – gestures you would pay money not to acquire. But a glitch in your brain has translated the 'don't' command into 'do' and it feels as though you're stuck with them anyway.

This phenomenon can happen at any stage in life. It could start when you are watching a colleague with a particularly annoying habit during business presentations or meetings, such as pen-twiddling or creating 'air-quotes', and are glad it's not in your repertoire. Then suddenly – to your horror – you find that it is. The only good things about these sudden unwanted mimic gestures is that they are relatively easy to stop.

The same cannot be said of the more long-range ones. These are all those annoying, depressing or downright embarrassing gestures, movements or expressions your parents used, those things that used to drive you mad as a kid. These 'signature' movements sit like a time bomb in your genes. Then one day, usually around middle age, you find you're doing them yourself. When your parents die the whole process progresses in leaps and bounds. Shaking these habits off is very, very difficult. For one thing, you may not even be aware you're doing them until a member of your family pipes up: 'You looked just like your father when you did that!'

4. Learned skills

These are the sets of movements we make a conscious effort to learn as part of a new skill. Driving, for instance, takes a new set of body language knowledge. So does something as simple as plugging in a kettle. If we work on these necessary sets of movements we acquire muscle memory, which means we can do them virtually without conscious thought and then – potentially – become very good at them. We may also be forced to modify gestures or posture because of bad health or physical damage.

You have control over all these four types of bodytalk, even though changing some can be more difficult than others. Always remember, you *can* change your behaviour, even if you can't alter your intrinsic personality. Body language is not uncontrollable, apart from the entirely involuntary tics that some people suffer from.

All you need to do to change is exert some control. Show your body who's boss for a change. Focus the conscious brain on the subconscious actions and press the override button.

▶ Basic Improvements

Your Body Posture Blueprint

Now you know a little more about bodytalk, we're going to start from basics by doing a sort of warm-up work-out.

Exercise

Start by standing in a relaxed position, feet a little less than shoulder-width apart and arms down by your sides. Now:

1. Stand tall. Stretch your spine. Imagine there is a string running through your spine and out through the top of your head, and that someone is pulling that string from the ceiling.

2. Roll your shoulders forward, in a slight hunch, then up in a circle and then back and down. This should straighten your shoulder posture without giving you a 'military' stance.

3. Shake your arms a little to relax your hands.

4. Do the same with your legs.

5. Focus on your shoulder dynamics. Close your eyes and take all the energy in your body and shift it into the shoulder area. Feel yourself growing in the shoulder and chest area. Do not puff your chest out, just see that area as your 'energy source'.

6. Now think down to your feet. This is the point where your energy touches the ground. Never become 'rooted', or you will give the appearance of overall negativity and lack of drive. Imagine your shoulder energy to be what is keeping your body in the air. Imagine it could hold you so that you could float above the ground if you wanted. See your feet as the connectors between your body and the ground, but don't see them as the parts of your body that are carrying all its weight.

   Now make sure your feet are straight and that your body is aligned down the middle of the feet. Balance yourself. Are you standing on the outside/inside edges of your feet? Is there too much emphasis on the ball or the heel of the foot? Correct any imbalance.

7. Breathe well. Air should be taken right through to the lower lungs, so that the stomach expands and contracts as you inhale and exhale. Imagine the oxygen is revitalising your body and that by exhaling deeply you are expelling all the negativity from your body. Balance your breathing. Don't take sudden deep breaths, just build on what you were doing naturally, only slow it a little.

8. Imagine your face is about to be ironed out. Do you want the creases ironed in or smoothed away? Remove the muscle tension from your face. Raise the eyebrows a little. Feel all the muscle tension in that area start to slacken. In business we tend to hold our brows in a permanent frown. Now raise your brows high and drop them a handful of times. When you raise them you should feel movement around the jaw area, too. Drop your brows to relax, but don't recrease them. Display the expression 'mild surprise'. Keep the brows very slightly arched and open your eyes a little more widely, too.

Imagine you are looking at someone you like very much, someone who makes you laugh. Act your response to that person with your eyes.

Push the tip of your tongue into the roof of your mouth to release jaw tension. Allow your teeth to part but keep your lips together. Now close your teeth. Pout your lips and then pull them back into a rictus grin. Relax the mouth into its normal closed position.

Raise your chin slightly, but keep your gaze where it was. Smile a little without showing your teeth. Smile with your eyes.

Self-talk

Now is the time to create a 'mantra' phrase, which you are going to repeat to yourself to charge yourself up. This works, but you need to learn to do it with a straight face. It's OK – I wouldn't ask you to do anything I wasn't prepared to do myself, honest.

Write your own script but make it short, sharp and easy to repeat. Words work on the subconscious by sound and tone as well as content, so you may even choose something that sounds calming or uplifting in preference to something that means exactly the same but sounds less soothing to your ear.

Some examples:

'I feel calm, confident and in control.'

'I am the greatest.'

'I am full of energy and positivity.'

'I shine like a light.'

'Seize the day.'

'I choose energy, power and enthusiasm.'

'I am as big as the challenge before me.'

'I am as omnipotent as Bill Gates, even though I don't have his cash flow.'

Whatever your mantra is, make sure it turns you on. If you are not a great lyricist, then thumb through the piles of books of life-enhancing quotes they keep near the till in most bookshops. You're bound to find one that does it for you. Don't worry about feeling ridiculous – no one else will know this is your phrase. Share it with colleagues or pals and the magic will vanish.

Now, as the final part of your work-out:

9. Breathe in and allow the mantra to run through your entire body.

10. Laugh out loud. Put your hands on your hips and roar. Go for it. One ear-splitter will do, but a volley is even better. A near-genuine laugh is best, but a theatrical one along the lines of a pantomime villain won't hurt either. Smiling and laughing do wonderful things to your body. And if your job's fatally dreary at least you'll have had one good laugh each day.

That is your core bodytalk work-out. You're going to use it at the start of every day and at key moments during the working day – although you will obviously use the abridged version *(see below)* at work, to avoid startling colleagues!

▶ Quick Fixes

Now for some quick-fix techniques:

Posture

This work-out is intended to revitalise your posture. Do it when you feel yourself going into screen-saver mode.

- If you are sitting at your desk, do the spine stretch (slowly and carefully, you don't want to pull anything), shoulder-roll and breathing.

- Pull your posture into alignment. Keep the weight even on both buttocks. Place your feet lightly on the floor, evenly spaced. Arch your back slightly, then relax it.

The Walk

I love a good walk. It is the best way to project yourself and the ultimate show-stopper if you get it right.

Exercise

- Again, begin with the basic posture-corrector.

- Bring your arms down to your sides, but never allow them to become rigid. Your palms should face your body and your fingertips should almost brush the sides of your legs. (Muscle-bound characters may find this impossible. So be it. I wouldn't start an argument over it. For one thing you sound too big to fight with.)

- Your arms are going to swing a little as you walk, so have a quick sway now, to practise.

- Tilt your pelvis in and slightly under. The angle of tilt will have to depend on sex (*which* sex you are, not how much you have). A woman can tilt her pelvis forward, tucking her bottom under, and look elegant when she walks. A man doing this might look like a contestant in a drag-queen pageant. Men might just concentrate on de-arching the spine, keeping a straight pelvis, instead.

- Let your feet do all the work when you walk. This means wearing the right type of shoes. The soles need to be flexible and the entire shoe must be comfortable and easy to keep on. A model will have to walk well in any style of shoe – platforms, slingbacks, flip-flops, hiking boots – but you can stick to a good pair of work shoes with a slim sole.

- The perfect size of pace will depend on your height. Small people often try to propel themselves along faster by employing bigger steps, but this looks stupid. Ditto tall gangly types who mince about. Walk from side to side in front of a mirror or video until you've got something that looks balanced to your physique.

▶ If you are having trouble with this, stand front-on to the mirror again and spread your stride until your feet are about shoulder-width apart. Now, keeping your feet at the same point, swivel on your toes until you are facing sideways. That should give you a good pace 'blueprint'. Keep working on it until you have consigned the pace to your muscle memory.

Your walk is going to be smoothly co-ordinated as you propel yourself along. Your torso is going to be relatively still, apart from a slight swing of the arms which will be caused by body movement, rather than a 'marching' style.

You probably lead with your head when you walk, and even more so when you are in a hurry. Head and shoulders are the easiest to propel, while everything else follows along in their wake. This gives a tortoise-like appearance, however. You can rectify this by leaning back slightly. Propel yourself from your feet and let the top half of your body enjoy the ride. Keep your weight on the back foot every time, placing your front foot heel-down and only moving your weight on to it as you start the change-over between back and front foot.

Never let your arms get too stiff at your sides, or dangle in front of your body.

Never stare at the ground unless it is absolutely vital for life and limb. Look up and look around you as you walk.

Eye Level

Eye contact in business should be interested and friendly, rather than threatening. You can practise by rehearsing with friends. Look them in the eye when you are listening. Hold the gaze when possible, but make sure you soften the expression to avoid a stare. Ask a question and hold the eye contact until you have the answer, but without looking challenging.

Also make eye contact when you are introduced to people and when you are listening in a group, especially when you are not participating verbally in the discussion. Choose certain moments to lean forward as you listen, holding your gaze.

If you feel yourself beginning to stare at someone, looking from one eye to another may help break up the gaze a bit, but if your eyes are large this device could be too obvious. Actors often look at the brows or forehead when they are in a close conversational pose, but this will just look weird in real life. A quick glance around the face may appear natural as a 'breaker', but avoid focusing on the other person's nose. This will bring on paranoia, as will staring at the ears or hairline.

Looking from the eyes to the mouth is necessary in communication as we do tend to lip-read, even when our hearing is good. Never overdo this, though. Your colleague may think you're flirting or that they have spinach between their teeth.

Gestures

Gestures will vary from person to person. How much do you use your hands in a natural, relaxed conversation? Be careful about editing this inherent style too much or you will look and feel awkward.

As a general point, though, avoid the over-use of 'barrier gestures' when you want to communicate or get your point across. When you fold your arms you appear to remove yourself from the communication. Sitting back in your seat with your arms folded and your gaze on the floor is one of the easiest ways to offend a speaker. The other is to look at your watch or yawn or shuffle papers while they are talking.

While you are speaking, you can employ open hand gestures or other hand movements to illustrate or add emphasis to your words. These can be a visual aid to your verbal outpourings.

Folding your arms is a barrier gesture that can discourage communication.

Remember to police the 'leakage', though – avoid fiddling and flapping movements that will steal the authority from your words.

Also avoid getting into a state of permanent over-dramatising.

In a bid to become great orators, politicians often place too much verbal and visual inflection on virtually every word that issues from their mouths. This is like an actor playing Thomas the Tank Engine in the style of Hamlet. Impassioned oratory is out of fashion at present. The public prefers people to tone down and 'tell it like it is', and the same should apply to your own gesticulating style. There is no need to form a fist and smack it into your palm every time you confirm you want sugar in your tea. Even your company's best product or latest mission statement probably doesn't merit the massive hand-waving and constipated facial expressions some speakers add as endorsement when they are presenting to other staff or clients.

Comfort Touches

Comfort touches are relatively insignificant and often subtle gestures and actions that increase our sense of well-being. Many of them stem from childhood. We all need to do these some of the time, and some of us need to do them all of the time. Often we are only aware we are doing them when someone brings it to our attention or the subject comes up and we trawl our subconscious to remember what we do.

The problem with comfort gestures is that they can deliver the message that you are in some way uncomfortable and in need of reassurance. If you are sitting in the comfort of your own home, they will rarely cause a problem, but in business they can be hugely undesirable.

Some examples of comfort gestures:

▶ Hair touching
This will often mean stroking or twiddling the hair. Stroking is the equivalent of stroking an animal's fur and is seen as a self-calming gesture, implying an inner build-up of anxiety. Hair-twiddling is an obvious throwback to childhood and looks just that: childish and immature.

Hair ruffling is different. It implies disorganised thought. Running the hand through the hair signals confusion and/or anxiety over a decision.

▶ Ear touching

Ears are a common comfort point. Pulling or rubbing the ear lobe is a calming gesture associated with decision-making, almost as though the act itself will help the decision process. It can give the impression that you are choosing your words carefully to the point of lying or that you have heard enough when the other person is speaking.

Ear poking, scratching or cleaning can signal lack of physical self-awareness due to anxiety or it can signal utter arrogance, like any unsavoury bodily act performed in front of an audience. The implication is that you either don't know you're doing it (nerves) or that you don't care (total lack of respect).

▶ Face touching

Touching the face when you are speaking is usually done to reassure yourself. We do it when we are shocked by something, touching fingers to cheek or lips, or we touch the mouth or chin to help ourselves out when we are speaking. Nose touching can signal insecurity, almost as though we like to check it is still there in the middle of our face. Eye-rubbing helps us stall for time, while showing that we don't really like what we are going to have to say next. Brow touching or rubbing will usually mean we are trying to massage the brain into increased output.

Unfortunately, face touching usually signals insincerity or even lying to the viewer. It can be seen as an attempt to 'mask' the words we are speaking, as though we are nervous about letting them come out of our mouths.

Mouth touching can also be a flirting signal. Placing the fingers on an erogenous zone like this can seem to imply you would like the listener to kiss you.

▶ Neck touching

Like the mouth, the neck can either signal sex or nerves. Tentative touching or rubbing will look tense and fluttery. Stroking the back of the neck will suggest mounting anxiety that you are trying to calm. Stroking the front will look flirty in a woman. In a man it implies shaving rash.

Shoulder rubbing

This shows anxiety, though bare-shoulder rubbing in women will be flirty.

▶ Body hugging

Any self-embrace, like folded arms hugged close to the torso, will imply a big need for self-reassurance *(see drawing 2, page 150)*. Some women speak with the arms from shoulder to elbow tucked in close to the sides of the body. This will imply a desire to be liked and a need for reassurance.

▶ Hand-wringing

Again, this shows anxiety and a desire to please. Done slowly it can signal building anticipation for mutual enjoyment; quickly, it tends to show fawning grovelling.

▶ Fiddling with jewellery

Necklaces, rings, watch-straps, ties – fiddling with any of these will give the impression of distress, nervousness, worry or covering up a mistake.

▶ Chewing hair or nails

Extreme nervousness.

▶ Fiddling in pockets or carrying documents across chest

Anxious. Something to hide. Attempting to cover up.

▶ High-folded arms in a woman or 'fig-leaf pose' in a man

Looks sexually threatened *(see drawing 3, page 150 and drawing 10, page 138)*.

▶ Legs crossed with top one swinging

This will look like impatience, as though you want to be rid of the person you are with.

▶ Finger-tapping or drumming

Ditto. A request to the other person to shut up.

▶ Foot-tapping or leg-quivering

Either extreme nervousness or impatience. This can signal you have a desire to do something urgently, like go to the loo.

▶ Finger-steepling

High status-signalling.

▶ Drumming steepled fingers together

Dictatorial. You want to see the other person squirm.

▶ Pen usage

Doodling – makes you look bored and distracted.
Tapping – irritating and irritated.
Twirling – nervous and compulsive.
Chewing – highly anxious.

Making a Point

Emphatic gestures will help reinforce your verbal and tonal messages. However, they should never be turned into an art form. Some people, like Tony Blair, have extended their emphatic repertoire to the point where the hands become the message. Looking as though you are doing signing for the deaf, however, will mean your hands have become a distraction, rather than enhancing your speech.

Gestures should never be allowed to upstage words because in a way they already do, even when they are subtle. Use your hands to enhance your message as follows:

▶ Keep hands open when you start to speak. Clutching, rubbing or wringing gestures look as though you are trying to edit your speech and stop yourself from saying what you think.

▶ Pointing and baton gestures will look aggressive, but do not have to be banned (*see drawing 1, overleaf*). Remember the power of the cluster signals. Smiling and pointing together will rarely offend. Stabbing and frowning may, though.

▶ Avoid metronomic gestures that last longer than three beats or you will look bossy and dictatorial.

▶ Be careful with the dismissive wave. Offensive enough in response to another's comments, it can look grade 'A' stupid when accompanying your own viewpoint.

▶ Making a fist can work if used to emphasise one major point. Use it too much, though, and you will look like a hideous child throwing a permanent tantrum.

Denial Gestures

These will undo the business message for you completely. They usually take the form of micro-gestures, although they can be larger. They often emerge at the end of a statement, rendering it invalid in the eyes of the audience. Sometimes they are used deliberately, to signal the message is corporate but not one that the speaker believes in personally.

You may, for example, give a serious message to your staff and then allow yourself a small half-smile at the end. Your eyes may flit to the ceiling and back. One eyebrow may raise. You could do the 'mouth shrug' (*see below*), curving your lips in a downward

A baton gesture can be aggressive.

A 'mouth shrug' combined with eyes raised to the ceiling will undermine your message.

arc, or your hands might open quickly into an 'if you like' finger shrug, flipping out and then back again at lightning speed.

As a child you became good at reading these denial gestures because parents use them a lot. Examples are the quick wink at the end of a telling-off or the softening of the facial expression that says the punishment is threatened, rather than meant.

When you use denial gestures as an adult, remember you are talking to a load of ex-children who will monitor these micro-gestures very accurately. The effect on your communication is like taking a big duster and erasing all the words on the chalkboard.

So, hang on at the end of your speech. A denial gesture at this point will show lack of faith or belief in your message. Is this what you want to show? If not, just pause and choose stillness instead.

Key Points in a Nutshell

▸ Start to study and improve your own body language by working on all six key areas.

▸ Be aware of your own comfort gestures. What are your regular habits? What happens when you are under stress? See if any of these gestures need modifying.

▸ Beware of denial gestures.

Chapter 5

*B*odytalk Strategies to Take You to the Top

So, WHAT IF your career goal is to get to the top, whether of your department, firm or own global empire?

There is a natural process of choosing a leader in a pack and most managers know this. This is why most business leaders fall into one of two groups:

1. The inspirational leader who inspires loyalty and confidence because staff believe that person knows what they are doing and that they are doing the right thing.

2. The leader who assumes the title minus the natural authority or consensus of the staff and is forced to engage in vigorous 'power-posturing', i.e. reminding everyone via words and deeds who is the boss and resorting to the 'do it because I say so' form of persuading and influencing.

Unfortunately Leader 1 is as rare as hen's teeth. Leader 2 is a lot more common. Employees tend to watch Leader 2 and use them as a role-model when they become leaders, passing the bad seed down through the generations like some genetic abnormality.

There is a Leader 3 as well. These are the ones who realise they have no natural leadership ability and so render themselves invisible. They spend their entire day in meetings and only emerge at the Christmas party, running the firm or department the rest of the time by proxy via their PA. Eventually the PA becomes like Norman Bates from the film *Psycho* and staff suspect the leader is in fact decomposing on a rocking chair in the attic somewhere, just like Norman's mother.

▶ Learn the Look

Whatever your current job title, you can look like a leader by high-status behaviour. Never fall into the trap of believing you have to wait until the job has been given to you before going through the motions. Some people just exude authority and most of it is done with bodytalk. None of it happens at birth. All of the techniques can be learned.

Visual power and authority tend to come from four bodytalk sources:

1. Size

This is a throwback to more prehistoric times when people physically fought their way to the top. And I do mean physically. Hopefully you gain promotion in your company by other means, but size can still be used to advantage.

A lot of powerful leaders have been shrimps, but tall people do have the advantage of standing out in a crowd. Unfortunately this often makes them shy, which means they refund nature's gift of inbred authority, preferring to look lanky, gawky and sit at the back of rooms to try and be invisible.

2. Stance

Whatever their size, leaders do tend to sit and stand higher. Some famous shrimpy leaders seemed taller than they were because they stood so well. They stretched up and squared up. Status can be shown through the shoulders. Rounded or sloping says you lack energy and delegate power. Squared shoulders imply the power comes from within. Walk and stand well and people around you will appear to 'catch' that energy, too.

3. Satellites

High-status people often come surrounded by satellites. These are the fawning hangers-on who act as role-models for the rest of the world. 'This is how I am to be treated' is what the leader is telling the rest of the workforce/world. Satellites also serve as an unofficial bodyguard, ensuring the leader is never spoken to by the lower ranks.

4. Space

High-status *in situ* means space. Leaders lead from a higher chair or a stage or podium. As I said earlier, the bigger the office, the bigger the boss. This is why open-plan offices that include a desk for the boss cause so much internal distress among the higher ranks. Being visible all day *and* without the trappings of power means they need to resource other ways of looking or sounding 'boss-like'. The trouble with leadership skills is that they are not always visible. Leaders lead. In among the others in an open-plan office the onus is upon them to be seen to be *doing* something. Once they start 'doing' something, like tapping on a keyboard, they are working, rather than leading. Perhaps they do need to be put back in their offices with their big windows and chairs.

Use of space is an important factor in status. In the Seventies and Eighties bosses of the 'command and control' school used space and furniture to create a feeling of power. They had the biggest offices, with the longest walks to get to their desks. The psychology behind this was simple: it reminded us of our first lesson in external power and authority at school. The old triggers still work.

▶ Power-posturing

Here are some tips on looking high-status. You can do what you like with them. I don't intend to moralise. If you want to come across as Attila the Hun, then go ahead, although I suggest you read a good book on leadership before you do. It's always better to take an informed decision, rather than just seizing all the power you can get because you were bullied at school and have a burning need to get your own back on the rest of the world. Of course businesses – and even countries – have been run as dictatorships, sometimes even with a degree of success, depending on your viewpoint. I'd still like you to study the alternatives, though, or, to use one of my favourite phrases: 'Don't make your selection until you've gone the full length of the counter.'

Desk Arrangement

Status comes with the confrontational style of desk arrangement, so that you sit facing someone else with a sheet of varnished walnut or mahogany between you. (Darker woods imply higher status, by the way.) This pose is, of course, absolutely useless for the more nurturing, coaching manager, as it creates a climate of confrontation and in some cases perceived aggression. It will not put people on the receiving end at their ease, unless you already have the reputation of being a draconian character, in which case your victim may prefer to have a wide desk between you as a safety barrier.

This may also apply at interviews where the candidate has no prior knowledge of your style of leadership, but feels the need of a comfort shield nevertheless.

The high-status desk should not be cluttered. Clutter implies lots of work of the practical kind and bosses don't do much of that. It also suggests cluttered, muddled thinking. Tidy up big-time. Be especially careful to bin old post-it notes and any toys or playthings you may be using for decoration.

God-like Auras

Then there is the age-old trick of positioning your chair in front of the window so that your back faces the light. This ensures visiting colleagues are forced to speak to your silhouetted form edged with a god-like halo of light. You may think I'm joking about this, but I'm not.

I worked with one company where the MD was almost endowed with superhuman powers. His staff swore he had a presence that you could feel before you could see him. Of course they were right – you *could* sense the guy when he arrived in the room. But take away the old wives' tales and the techniques were easy:

1. He kept his appearances down to a minimum. Therefore his visits seemed special.

2. He would always choose a time when the office was pretty crowded but not too busy.

3. He entered through a door that was visible to some of the staff via their peripheral vision. So some people *did* see him come in. It was the effect that had on their body language (a certain stiffening and alertness of posture) that was sensed by the rest of the pack, not his appearance as such.

No special magic, then. But it was an excellent bodytalk trick.

Power Seating

Do you want the seat of power? Literally? It pays to work out in advance which it is.

If you are at a meeting at a long conference table then the obvious choice is at one of the two ends. Pick the wrong end by accident and you're dead in the water, though, so a quick recce of the room beforehand is to be advised. The person who sits at the end furthest from the leader is either in direct conflict or about to be got rid of, or both. Often the board table is so huge that anything they say will be inaudible, anyway. Even if it is as clear as a bell, the power-posture boss at the other end can pretend not to have heard it.

In some cases, though, the power seat will be in the middle of the board table, especially if the chair then faces the door. This is the 'Last Supper' pose. You may even find subordinates not sitting on the opposite side at all.

By sitting in the middle you make the two people who take the more obvious power seats at either end of the table look like jerks or even bookends, as they are forced to spend the entire meeting leaning inward to hear what you are saying, especially if you are deliberately softly spoken. Never take this seat and try this tactic if you are of lower status, though, as you will end up making your own boss feel like a prat.

The other power pose is to sit in the least likely seat at a meeting. You deliberately pick a low-status chair – i.e. near the far end or half-behind a door – and sit back with your chin resting on your steepled fingertips. This 'delegation of authority' routine scares other employees witless. You look like an ideal boss, i.e. one who allows your staff some slack and lets them have a voice in keynote meetings, without making interruptions. The reality is that your presence is more overpowering than if you were on your feet shouting the odds. You become as omnipresent as the father who sits in the kitchen at a teenagers' party. Your body language means you are still firmly in control. By giving staff no clues to your opinions, though, you dangle them helpless in deep water, without their rubber ring.

Nothing is worse than the boss who says they will attend, but not join in. Staff like comments, nods and body language signals at meetings to reassure them they are running on the right lines.

Follow My Leader

A natural pattern of most packs is that the leader instigates a change of pose and the rest of the pack follows along a few moments later. This is all to do with 'on the hoof' packs who need a leader to decide where to wander. The same applies to the human pack, particularly in business.

So, spotting the real leader or decision-taker in a sales meeting, for instance, used to simply be a matter of monitoring this ongoing game of 'follow my leader' and spotting the instigator. That would be the first one to relax, sit back or forward in the chair, or even study their watch. Things are a tad more complex in work these days and the formula has to be less precise. Several factors could be scuppering the process:

1. Because of the new style of leadership skills, involving a much lower profile set of competencies, no one in the group may be aware exactly who their leader is, even the leader themselves. Modern job titles do little to help this situation.

2. The decision-taker may not be the group leader. In a buying situation the final say will often rest with someone from accounts who normally barely sees the light of day.

3. You may be looking at a group with an identity crisis. Many people have read about the 'first to change pose' wheeze and are keen to wrest power by trying it out. Groups like these are always interesting to observe, as the results are often hilarious. Each person vying for the top job tries to get in first with the body alterations until the whole group looks as though it has taken speed. In these scenarios look for the person who is barely moving at all. That will probably be the real leader chilling out.

Power-dressing

You will probably know all about this already, because you either did it in the Eighties or have read about it since and seen the footage of Margaret Thatcher in her prime. Power dressing was extremely effective. It reached its height with the film *Wall Street* and its nadir with the movie *Working Girls*, where Melanie Griffiths found promotion thanks to little more than a back-combed hairdo and a can of lacquer.

Clothes have always been used to exhibit status, though, and always will, despite recent attempts to down-dress the troops. Certain colours imply power just as others imply you're a wimp. Navy, black, charcoal, white and deep red will all suggest status. They are a business cliché but a cliché that always works. Earthy-looking browns, greens, creams and beiges suggest a less corporate profile. Strong tones, like purple, emerald, dark pink and blue, go in and out of fashion as business colours but create a raised profile. Baby pink, pale blue, lemon and pistachio look cute and passive.

Big shoulders were the power-dresser's signature and although huge padding has gone out of fashion, the tailored shoulder still tends to look more high-status than less structured lines. The perceived link between uniform and status is a hard one to break. The suit looks like a uniform. The cardigan just doesn't say the same thing, somehow.

Many bosses dress like slobs, but whatever you are wearing, if you are dressing for high-status, the clothes should fit and move well. At the very least your outfit will need to look unremarkable. If your tie is crooked and your shoes grubby or worn or your buttons too tight then people will notice.

Down-dressing has created a nightmare power situation. Because there is little in a pair of chinos and a sports shirt to suggest status, the emphasis is firmly on body language to provide the clues – except in Oriental businesses, where they tend to assume the oldest person present is the most senior.

Posture

The true high-status character will not have to attract attention, they will tend to command it. Standing tall is important and so is keeping your head up. The angle of tilt can be crucial, though. Tilt your head too far back and you will appear arrogant. Drop it too low and you'll look bashful. A level gaze is best.

Walking at speed but never rushing is vital. The walk should look co-ordinated and you should learn to do it with your arms hanging at your sides. Creating arm or hand 'barriers' while you walk will make you appear defensive, rather than in control.

Tilting back in your chair can imply an air of rakishness that some people equate with status. The precariousness of the position when speaking across the desk suggests firm control in extreme situations. The complete power-posturer will add to the effect by sticking their hands behind their head (*see overleaf*). This armpit-baring routine is psychologically fascinating. When an animal wants to signal submission to a stronger enemy it will often do so by displaying the most delicate body parts. A cat, for example, will lie on its back with its belly exposed to show an end to a fight. This manoeuvre is generally unpopular in business for the obvious reason that signals can get confused, and lying on the floor belly-up could easily be misconstrued as something more sexual. So we show the palms of the hands instead.

By this token 'armpitting' should signal submission or weakness, but it doesn't. What it does show is arrogance. It tells the person opposite that you are no perceived threat at all, which

This is the ultimate power-posturer position.

can be unflattering, even between close friends. As a business gesture it is very rude. Real power-freaks take this display one step further by then placing their feet upon the desk. This is totally arrogant. In signalling terms it is the equivalent to a boxer dropping their guard to imply the opponent couldn't punch their way out of a wet paper bag. Don't go there.

Strong-arm Tactics

Hands play a major part in the power-display. Using them as a barrier can appear negative and so of course will indulging in fiddling and other anxiety or comfort signals. Hand-wringing will be low-status, but certain types of hand-folding can be high.

Hands that are interlinked via the fingers only will tend to veer towards the high-status. If you sit with your hands in front of you on the desk and the fingers evenly meshed you will give the appearance of being calm and in control. If you raise the meshed hands by propping your elbows on the chair arms, the air of superiority is heightened. If you then steeple the fingers, you begin to look judgemental and in total control (*see opposite*). All

Steepling fingers can appear judgemental.

you need to do next is peer over the tops of your spectacles and you'll appear to be on the Attila the Hun end of the power scale.

The Power Shake

In the Eighties, one great feature of power-posturing was the business power-shake. Legend had it that the person who got their hand on top exhibited the more power. So the idea was to either twist as you shook or approach with your hand held out nearly horizontal, palm-downward, to force your 'opponent' into the weaker position. This was popular at the time and some sad souls still use it now.

The newer version just has to be 'the bone crusher', which is no more subtle than it sounds. Here you employ a grip so hard you make the other person wince. This somehow shows strength and superior status. I have shaken hands with many truly high-status people, though, and not one of them has felt the need to crush my knuckles to prove who they are.

Status Staring

Eye contact plays a part in any high-status display. It makes you look confident and a good listener. Overdoing it is not a sign of power, though, but of madness. As I stated earlier, too much eye contact looks like either lust or war. So, use eye contact all the time when you are listening, but vary it slightly when you are talking, or you will overpower someone in the worst way.

Rudeness

Being rude to colleagues is often seen as a sign of power, probably because only a boss could get away with rude behaviour without getting punched on the nose. But rudeness is another trait I have rarely encountered in people who have genuinely got to the top. People with true power don't have to be rude to prove it. Rudeness comes from those who either haven't got it but want it or who have got it but deep down don't feel they merit it.

Space Invasion

We spoke earlier about the territorial zones and personal spatial awareness. Invading a colleague's territory is horrible, nasty, petty-minded power-posturing, because it makes them feel uncomfortable. Bad bosses stand and read over an employee's shoulder while they're working and then wonder why they make mistakes. Looming over someone is an act of aggression, whether you meant it that way or not.

If you really want to cause grief, you can play the 'I'll stand and you sit' game for hours. By standing while the other person sits you can look superior, or even threatening, unless you are in any way 'performing' for that person, i.e. selling, persuading or being in any way assessed, in which case the sitter will assume the superior role.

Chair height and size become important if you both choose to sit. The big leather chair versus the small functional kind will say boss v. subordinate. This is enhanced if the leather one has swing or rock facilities and the other chair is static. The worst-case scenario for the victim is the armless chair. Sitting opposite a lounger while your own elbows remain unpropped virtually forces you into low-status bodytalk. The only fight-back gambit at your disposal at that point will be to prop one elbow on the back of the chair in a devil-may-care manner. This can turn pear-shaped, though, if the back of the chair is too high or too sloping to make the move feasible and you are forced into a retreat.

One company I work with has what it calls its 'unpreferred supplier' chair. This is one of the height-adjustable office models, only the adjuster mechanism has broken, so that as you sit in the chair you slowly sink. This comical chair-lowering is a subtle humiliation for suppliers who have let the company down in some way.

One final point on space invasion – if you accept a tea or coffee and then find there is nowhere to place it, you can consider yourself woefully out-manoeuvred by a put-down expert and potential psychotic.

The Wannabes

If you want to raise your status at work in a positive way, sow the seeds for promotion with some of these quick tips:

▸ Always look smart and well-groomed.

▸ Carry yourself well. Look comfortable in your own skin.

▸ Walk with determination but never rush.

▸ Give a good handshake.

▸ Use people's names when you talk to them.

▸ Look interested when people talk to you, even if you are busy.

▸ Learn how to close down the time-wasters tactfully.

▸ Position yourself well at meetings.

▸ Keep an uncluttered desk.

▸ Avoid fiddling gestures, like playing with jewellery or pens.

▸ Avoid comfort gestures, like hair-stroking or twiddling or pen-sucking.

▸ Avoid dumbing-down behaviour, like giggling or disgusting baby-talk.

▸ Sit and stand in a balanced fashion. Leg-crossing is OK when you are sitting, but arm-folding is less useful. Standing with your arms folded can look completely masterful, though, if done well.

▶ Face people front-on when communicating with them and employ confident eye contact.

▶ Smile when appropriate, but avoid the over-stretched 'social' smile that can look false. Constant smiling will look weak.

▶ Be charming and polite at all times. Good manners imply the lack of a chip on the shoulder. Prickly people are insecure.

▶ Be calm. This looks like confidence.

▶ Never be seen indulging in tacky office behaviour like gossiping or moaning.

▶ Indulge in frequent high-profile visits to other members of staff. Ask them how things are going and listen in a helpful manner. This is the sort of walk-the-job stuff proper leaders and managers should do. The good thing is you can do it under the guise of professional friendliness and still achieve a visual dress-rehearsal for the real thing.

▶ Never eat at your desk.

▶ If you are attending a works social event, like a leaving party, always leave early, before the bad behaviour starts.

Key Points in a Nutshell

▶ Decide on your level of ambition. In marketing terms it's never too early to know where you are going.

▶ Start to look the part as soon as possible. Never hide your visual light under a bushel. People tend to stereotype according to perceived image, especially in a large firm.

▶ Act the part.

▶ Show an interest in others. Raise your work profile in a positive way.

Chapter 6

Quick-fix Bodytalk Tips

HERE ARE A few business situations and some quick-fix bodytalk to get you through – or out – of them.

▶ How to 'Give Good Ear'

Listening is one of the most important communication skills. Nobody listens much in business, so colleagues and clients are easily charmed by anyone who manages to look attentive. Show good listening skills by:

▶ **Stopping working**
You may be able to do 10 jobs at once, but to the speaker you will appear rude or distracted if you carry on reading, typing or adding up figures.

▶ **Turning to face the speaker, front on**

▶ **Using constant eye contact**
Looking away, even for a nano-second, will make you look distracted, as though searching for something more interesting to do.

▶ **Tilting your head**
Tilt at a small angle for lively interest, a more radical angle for deep, aerobic listening when you are struggling to stay awake.

▶ **Raising an eyebrow**
It worked for Roger Moore in *The Saint* and it will work for you. The one-eyebrow raise registers a whole raft of emotions, from mild concern or surprise to rapt attention.

▶ **Putting your hand to your face**
Touching your knuckles against your chin is good. Propping one finger against your mouth is also OK, as it suggests silent listening. An index finger straight up against the side of the face can look fey or judgemental.

The head tilt shows interest, but the index finger position can look fey.

▶ **Nodding**

Nodding is good. If you do it too quickly and energetically, though, it will be seen as a sign that you are waiting to interrupt.

▶ **Mirroring**

Show empathy by 'mirroring' the speaker's pose and facial expressions (more on this later). Be careful, though, particularly with laughter. The British in particular have a habit of doing 'the brave laugh', while recounting personal tragedy. Laughing along while someone is telling you her husband has died is not a good way to bond with colleagues.

▶ **Keeping silent**

Keep quiet, even when the speaker has appeared to have finished. Allow a small time lapse. Still look interested, though. This may encourage them to tell you more. This is an invaluable ploy if you are working as an investigative journalist.

To avoid:

▶ **Over-responding**

People who get over-excited in response to rather dull workplace stories will usually be regarded as total phoneys who are actually paying no attention at all.

▶ **The 'parked' gesture**

When we find a place in someone's narrative where we want to join in we will often raise a finger or open our mouths, guppy-style. If the speaker refuses the attempted interruption we leave the gesture there, 'parked' for future use. This is not conducive to good conversation, as you are informing the speaker that anything they say after that point will be unheard.

▶ **Yawning**

Yes, of course you know yawning really is a *faux pas*, but it's happened to all of us, hasn't it? When you feel a yawn come on in the middle of listening you really have only two gambits at your disposal: you can either yawn without restriction and apologise, saying the room is stuffy, or you can try to smother it. This involves keeping your lips clamped shut while your face bloats out like a toad and your eyes start to water. It is my theory that the speaker will still be aware that you have yawned.

▶ **Looking at your watch**

A complete and utter stinker of a gesture, no matter how necessary at the time. There is no verbal route for digging yourself out of this hole.

▶ How to Look as Though You Know What You Are Doing

Busking your way through a job is rarely to be recommended, but it happens to even the greatest of us at some time or another. The received wisdom used to be to bluff your way out by changing the subject, waffling, throwing the question out to the rest of the group or simply pretending and hoping no one noticed. The trouble is that people do notice now, thanks in part to the rottweiler school of interrogating techniques that most TV and radio interviewers seem to have graduated from.

In the present climate, owning up to ignorance needs to be the first option. If you do so, you may even gain praise for your integrity. If this is your choice, go straight on to the next section on how to stall for time. Otherwise, if you plan to cover up your ignorance:

▶ Create a sense of physical calm. Move less during this period of total confusion, rather than more. Avoid any traces of apologetic body language like stooping or over-smiling.

▶ Keep your hands firmly clamped to the desk top. Otherwise they will give the game away big-time by flapping or fiddling.

▶ Use the word 'clarify' to stall for time. Don't say you don't understand, ask the other person to clarify what they have just said. Use their name as you address them. If you are still stumped after they have explained for the second time, pause and say, 'As in?'

Another useful phrase is: 'That's not what I've heard.' I write for a magazine that specialises in celebrity gossip and missing out on a bit of new scandal can be like committing professional suicide. When confronted with a unknown fact, the stock reply is: 'That's not what I've heard.' I have even heard a gutsy colleague use this when told a certain celebrity had died the day before.

▶ Avoid wild staring. These moments mainly occur during business presentations where you lose the plot or have no idea how to answer an audience question. The stare will either be aimed at the ceiling or at the flip chart or Light-pro screen. This makes it appear that you are expecting some sort of divine intervention. If you must stare, stare someone straight in the face. This will make them believe the onus is on them to speak or react, not you.

▶ Stand up. If you have been asked to do a desk-bound job that is a complete mystery to you, standing will at least look brave, if slightly quirky. Standing during a business presentation on a subject you know nothing about may also help. Showing keenness and a desire to communicate implies you have immense knowledge of the subject matter. If you start your talk but can't continue, they will then think you just dried, which can happen to any performer and is a sign of anxiety, rather than dumbness.

▶ Focus on looking more confident than you feel. Carry a pen and notebook and be seen to be jotting down notes when you do get directions, training and advice. That way colleagues will think you're learning, at least.

▶ Approach people for help positively, avoiding using over-apologetic words or body language. Be concise and clear with both forms of communication. Use eye contact when you talk and smile, rather than offering a worried expression.

▶ When someone gives you information, shut up and use the listening signals. Look focused and intense, rather than unsure and flappy.

▶ Never lurk around someone's desk when you need to ask for help. If they are busy on the phone, approach them confidently and then wait until you catch their attention and signal by tapping your watch and raising fingers to show that you will return in x-amount of minutes. (Raising the 'two-minute signal' is not to be recommended, for obvious reasons.) Alternatively, scribble the reason for your visit on a post-it note, plus the time that you intend to return, and place it on their desk. If they are busy working and refuse to halt for a second to acknowledge you, do the same thing regardless.

▶ To impress during induction, always take a seat near the front and make yourself visible, even if your knowledge of the subject matter is flimsy. As a rule, the less you know, the more visible you need to be. Trainers and lecturers aren't stupid, despite appearances to the contrary. They know the people sitting at the back of a room or group are trying to render themselves invisible. It is the trainer's job to bring those people out, so they invariably end up getting picked on more than the eager-beavers at the front.

▶ Screen-watch. Screen-savers are a godsend in terms of stalling when stumped at work. Use one that includes a lot of movement, so that your eye contact is genuinely active and you avoid the blank stare. If your screen faces away from the rest of the office and you keep your fingers resting lightly on or even moving across the keyboard you should manage to fool colleagues that you are working furiously, rather than suffering a major brain-blank. Pause occasionally and stroke or finger your chin. This gives the appearance of thinking intelligently. Purse your lips and frown a little, too. Avoid all signals of 'dumb thinking', like:

- staring at the ceiling
- falling slumped into your chair
- rocking or twisting your chair
- fiddling with jewellery
- biting your nails
- yawning

- groaning
- winding twists of hair
- picking your nose or a spot
- gazing round the office
- smiling or giggling
- chewing your pen
- gnawing your Styrofoam coffee cup or turning it into confetti
- tapping
- doodling
- whistling
- playing with change in a pocket
- trying to flip your mouse-mat like a beer mat
- cleaning your teeth with a finger
- picking a price label off the sole of your shoe
- playing computer games – people always know what you've been doing, no matter how quickly you turn the thing off
- playing with desk toys, especially retro ones, like a Newton's cradle
- staring out of the window
- staring at a blank wall.
- flossing your keyboard.

▶ Ways to Stall for Time Before You Speak at a Meeting or Talk

▶ Take off your glasses
This will only give you a nano-second, but it may be enough.

▶ Confer in a whisper with a colleague
Clinton used this technique to great effect the time his cue-board exhibited the wrong speech.

▶ Clean your glasses
This works especially well if you use a silk pocket handkerchief for the job. People will be so fascinated by your flamboyance that they will allow a gap of several seconds.

▶ Stand and stare

Once you have risen to your feet it is possible to engage the audience with a meaningful stare for at least 10 seconds before they begin to suspect you have suffered an interruption in your intellectual processes. Up until then they will think they've done something wrong themselves or that they are about to listen to something of major importance. It was the way your school head used to announce the fact that someone had done something unspeakable in the swimming-pool. (Always remember the old triggers work the best.)

▶ Light a pipe

I loathe this manoeuvre and am not suggesting you buy a briar if your only smoking to date has been a swift drag on a menthol behind the bike shed. I have, though, seen pipe smokers keep an audience in appalled thrall for many minutes while going through the filling, tamping, drawing and lighting process and, in one case, even pulling the stem off and inserting a pipe cleaner.

▶ Flatter the last speaker

This always works a treat, even if the words are laced with sarcasm or irony.

Don't stall for time by:

▶ clearing your throat

▶ pouring and drinking water

▶ shuffling through notes

▶ focusing your slides or the Power Point

▶ laughing nervously

▶ announcing you are not good at speaking to groups

▶ saying you are nervous

▶ cleaning your pen

▶ giving out handouts

- clapping the last speaker

- checking your flies multiple times

- buttoning your jacket or straightening your tie

- checking that your mobile is switched off and asking others to do the same

- knocking your chair over as you stand up

- cracking your knuckles

- going to the loo or asking if anyone else would like a comfort break

- asking if people would mind talking amongst themselves for a few moments

- asking if everyone can hear you OK

- rootling in your handbag

- or even – and I saw this with my own eyes – going round the entire group of 50, shaking hands first.

▶ Handling Mistakes

We all make mistakes from time to time in the workplace – anything from forgetting a colleague's name when making an introduction to a client to sending that private e-mail throughout the entire company by pressing the wrong button. We tend to be more troubled by these than we need to be. Our brains are normally full of information and concerns and it's not surprising that there is a little glitch now and again.

Tips for covering up mistakes:

- Keep relatively still. This will prevent a tendency to over-react because of embarrassment.

- Never back up a stupid deed with stupid body language. There is no need to bounce and dance about flapping your arms as if to celebrate the mistake.

▶ Do your best to appear otherwise intelligent. If you smile, keep your lips closed. Raise your eyebrows cynically and shrug slightly. If the mistake is a whopper, you could make a palms-up gesture with a slight, happy-looking shrug.

▶ One 'sorry' is always enough. Never try to explain further. Either you will dig a deeper hole or you will end up including the word 'stupid' or 'Alzheimer's' in your self-description, or both.

▶ Work on a buddy system. You and a buddy could each be on the alert for the other's error and cause a distraction asap.

▶ Eight Image Stereotypes to Avoid at Work

1. The Surrogate Mother

Nurturing is supposed to be high on every working girl's list of 'admirable qualities I bring to the job'. Although this is patently utter tosh, the stereotype survives and should not be encouraged.

Once the label of 'office nanny' gets pinned on you, consider yourself lumbered. You will be forced to wear cardigans each working day of your life and your routine will involve a constant round of organising baby showers and taking collections for people who are leaving. People like to be nannied, but not by their boss, so expect your chances of promotion to be less than negligible. To avoid this particularly ghastly tag:

▶ Never seize the tea pot and offer 'to be mother'. Prefer to sit still and die of dehydration.

▶ Clear your desk drawer of anything medical, practical or comforting, like plasters, headache tablets, spare tights, safety pins and sewing kits.

▶ Never take a collection for *anything*.

▶ If a colleague comes into your office for the use of a kindly ear, stand up immediately. Do not offer a seat. Look concerned (head cocked, troubled frown, hint of a smile), but stay on your feet.

▶ Never use baby-talk in the workplace. It sounds kind and brings out the dependent types.

▶ Use few 'closed' gestures. Arms folded across the bosom tends to look matronly, as does the front-rib under-bosom hand clutch.

▶ As you get older, develop a bit of a hard edge. For some reason people always expect older women to become nurturing souls. To avoid the 'surrogate mumsie' tag, make sure you look like no one's mother, apart – possibly – from Johnny Rotten's. Scowl a lot and swear on the odd occasion.

▶ Walk about a lot, which negates the illusion of comfort 'nesting' at your desk or workstation.

▶ If junior colleagues come to you for help because you are the fount of all knowledge, do not be unduly flattered. They are using you the way most of us use Spellcheck – because we're too lazy to learn while there's someone or something else around to do the job for us. Throw back questions in response, as in: 'Where's the paper kept for the photocopier?' 'Well, where do you suppose it's kept?' This is very much in the spirit of 'coaching' staff, rather than just telling them and is enormously trendy in business at the moment, so no one should accuse you of being rude.

▶ Never pat anyone.

▶ Have no kiddie bits around your desk, like photos of, drawings by or horrendous plasticine objects created by your children. When they get to the age and level of talent when they can paint like Van Gogh you can afford to frame a few of their pictures and hang them about, but not until then.

▶ Do not wear large lockets or brooches.

▶ Avoid scarves and cardigans.

▶ Show indifference to biscuits. Never be seen opening a packet up.

▶ Never be the one who pins up notices in the toilet saying things like 'Now please flush.'

2. The Company 'Card'

If 'the nanny' is invariably female, then 'the joker' is nearly always a male. Fun is good, but being labelled as the company joker is a bad career move, unless you happen to work for Billy Smart's Circus. If the sound of laughter means more to your ears than the sound of money going into your bank account then crack on with the image, but remember that people at work will often only laugh out of politeness or sheer exhaustion. Don't take a smile as a sign of approval. To avoid being seen as the office joker (or joke):

▶ Never wear funny clothes. Fashion can be witty, but comic socks and ties are the abattoir of style and taste. If they also play a tune, consider yourself about as amusing as a dose of herpes.

▶ Don't give colleagues nicknames. They may not like them and they might not share your 'wicked' sense of humour.

▶ Avoid truly ghastly catchphrases, especially ones filched off the telly. Used too often they can be like nails on a chalkboard for your colleagues.

▶ Try to avoid using sounds that carry all the way to the boss's office, like silly comic voices and an inane laugh.

▶ Strike a balance between your fun and serious sides. People need to know that you are capable of doing a good job of work and they won't if they start to doubt your sanity or are unsure when you are being serious and when you are taking the mickey.

▶ Avoid an array of comic objects around your desk.

▶ Never be the one to make the smart remarks at business meetings. A couple of up-front one-liners can break the ice, but a barrage of sarcasm and wit can be seen as time-wasting negativity.

▶ Sit at the front at meetings. The joker will traditionally lounge at the back, making their comic observations look like heckling.

▶ Try not to be highly animated when you speak. Clowns move around a lot to be funny. Dry humour works better in business as it implies intellect. Looking serious but being funny is much better for your career than looking funny but being stupid.

▶ Avoid long set-piece jokes at work. They are rarely really funny and colleagues tend to laugh out of pity, boredom or embarrassment. For most of them it is like faking an orgasm – they hope it will egg you on to finish earlier.

▶ Avoid 'Jack the lad' hairdos, like anything combed forward or over-gelled.

3. The Terminally Professional

If this is you, you are capable of making even the joker appear lovable. You are cold, bland and emotionless to the point of being a corpse in a suit. You are also currently in good company in business, as there are legions of you out there. Being professional is one thing, but now and again you do need to prove that you are not a hologram.

▶ Smile occasionally, especially when colleagues greet you. And leave the smile on your face for a little while. Terminally professionals tend to employ the 'lightning flash' smile, a quick spasm of the mouth muscles that is gone as quickly as it arrived.

▶ Make small-talk. Clients, in particular, have a dislike of being grilled straight away at meetings. Build a little rapport.

▶ Turn the handshake into something other than a combat zone. It is supposed to be an ice-breaking, not ball-breaking manoeuvre.

▶ Get to know your staff. Ask them about their families now and again. Buy them biscuits.

- ▶ Do something funny. Even once will do.

- ▶ Cut down on the use of jargon.

4. The Lurker

There is one of these hovering around every boss's desk, waiting to speak or plucking up courage to interrupt. They try to be barely visible during most of the working day, thereby making themselves oddly high-profile for all the wrong reasons. To avoid this:

- ▶ Never ever creep around the workplace. Walk with a sense of purpose, even if you're not sure where you're going.

- ▶ Make a good entrance. Never open a door gingerly or try to tiptoe into a meeting room.

- ▶ Never perch on the edge of a chair, especially your own.

- ▶ Stop using the word 'sorry', as in 'Sorry to bother you, but. . .'

- ▶ Don't dither. If you start to shake someone's hand or open a door for them or raise your hand to make a point at a meeting, then carry it through.

- ▶ Use more eye contact. If you catch someone's attention in this way they can respond if they are tied up and this prevents you having to lurk around their desk waiting for them to finish. Eye contact followed by a quick raise of the eyebrows will stimulate them to signal when they might be through. If they do stop talking to enquire why you are hovering, explain why.

- ▶ Smile less, especially at inanimate objects. Over-smiling can make you look nervous, docile and passive.

5. Dumb and Dumber

Dumbing-down is not a good career move and yet many do it on a regular basis, either to appear winsomely helpless or cute or to seem even dumber than their boss (a bit like deliberately losing at squash) or even as a manipulative gambit when giving orders or getting someone to do their work for them or to work overtime. Once you have dumbed-down, though, you have dug yourself a pit that you will never climb out of. You will never be seen as the intellectual sophisticate again.

Dumb and dumber is mainly a body language ploy. The hands are clutched in front of the body, either at rib-cage level or above the bosom. The face is either smiling coquettishly or pouting, which will warp the words with a childish lisp. The head might be tilted for extra effect. The body may sway or rock a little. Baby words emerge, like 'ickle' and 'oo'. The effect is like being drowned in treacle-soaked suet. To watch a mature woman go through this ritual in an attempt to cajole a colleague into doing a job for her is to fight the urge to produce projectile vomit.

Men dumb-down, too, often with the bewildered boy routine. One businessman I know pretends he has trouble choosing his own food, which leads to his PA running around filling his plate for him. She thinks she is helping him out on a tough call. He ends up looking as though he employs staff to do the most menial chores.

Avoid dumbing-down, however manipulative it can be, by:

▶ Always using proper, grown-up words.

▶ Never ever pouting, unless being outrageously, ironically flirty.

▶ Keeping your hands by your sides or in your pockets while you are making a request.

▶ Never using the words: 'Do me a favour.'

▶ Keeping your body static while making a request – never sway, never rock.

6 The Stress Junkie

Stress is part of the rich tapestry of modern business life. Some people suffer it bravely, trawling every known cure from Balsamic Yoga classes to macrobiotic flotation tanks in the quest for serenity and calm. Others merely thrive on the adrenaline buzz of constant anxiety, constantly massaging the old adrenal glands in an effort to achieve the maximum high.

Stress needn't be suffered in silence, but the stress junkie goes to the other extreme and broadcasts their symptoms to the biggest audience available. Their image is like Lloyd Bridges in *Airplane* – sleeves rolled up to the bicep, hair ruffled, constant pacing and fidgeting movements, plus a tendency to over-eat and over-inhale at speed. Gestures are uncoordinated, speech is rapid and clothes come from a chain of shops I have never discovered, but which obviously bears a name like 'Wired Geeks R Us'.

If you flaunt your stress in this way it can only be for one of three reasons:

1. You are truly into stress overdrive and near to cracking, in which case you have my genuine sympathy as this is obviously not a funny situation.

2. You are a complete drama queen.

3. You want to impress everybody by the amount of unstinting effort you put into your work. You assume the sight of your self-induced sweat will bring you admiration, pity and promotion.

If your motivation comes from one of the last two categories then you are deserving of pity, but not for the reasons you think.

Cool is good in modern business. It was only in the last century that flash and dash ever impressed. Drop all of the following habits immediately:

▶ puffing

▶ tutting

▶ muttering

▶ running about the workplace

▶ chewing your nails or any other part of your body

▶ obsessive fiddling with any part of your body

▶ constantly pushing your glasses up the bridge of your nose

▶ rolling your head around to loosen the neck muscles, *à la* Mike Tyson

- drumming your fingers

- wiping the sweat off your face with your hand

- pushing the same hand up through your hair to use sweat as hair mousse

- rolling up your sleeves and loosening your tie the minute you sit down to work

- swearing to yourself (or others, of course)

- that horrible little martyred laugh any time anyone asks you to do something

- kicking or otherwise hitting inanimate objects.

7. The Genuinely Stupid

Dumbing-down is one thing, but the point with the genuinely stupid is that they don't have to, because they're down there already. They have the attention span of a gnat and the memory of a goldfish. Their brain works to its own agenda and this is baffling to everyone, especially them. There are only two places in business for them: either at the very top or the very bottom of the company. If they are aware of their own stupidity, their company probably copes quite well. If they have intellectual pretensions, though, they are in deep trouble. To prevent being thought of as genuinely stupid, avoid:

- showing off about hangovers

- showing off your body piercing

- sticking embarrassing objects around your PC screen

- head-banging or playing air-guitar while you work

- making up hateful nicknames for other colleagues

- using so much jargon that you appear to be speaking a foreign language

- starting each day with the same grinding clichés, for example, 'Another day, another dollar'

- pretending you've just woken up when someone asks you a question

- acting on your own initiative – get things checked and double-checked.

8. The Pike

This label is a reference to the fact – real or manufactured, I don't know – that if you put a pike into a tank with guppies, the pike will eat the smaller fish. Put a sheet of clear glass between the two and it will soon learn it can't get to them. Take the sheet away and it won't try because it has learnt to expect failure.

Pikes are the cynics in business. Age and experience has not taught them wisdom, just caution and negativity. They greet new ideas with derision. If it didn't work when it was tried before, they can see no reason for giving it another go.

In order not to be seen as a pike (even if you are one), avoid:

- slumping in your seat at meetings

- starting sentences with: 'Yes, but . . .'

- sighing or tutting

- rolling your eyes heavenwards

- shaking your head while looking downward

- folding your arms in a pose of total denial

- yawning

- making a presentation with your hands stuffed into your trouser pockets

- looking unnecessarily old by wearing baggy, shapeless suits, old-fogey ties, brooches and assorted knitwear

- phrases like 'in my day' or 'of course, you'll all be too young to remember that'

- growing grey or white facial hair

▶ wearing the same style of spectacles for years.

Now you know the various types of image it is especially important to avoid, let's consider how you might want to come across to your colleagues.

▶ How to Look Assertive

Since the term was first coined in the Seventies we've all wanted to be more 'assertive' in the workplace, that is, neither aggressive nor passive but effective, full of integrity and able to stand up for ourselves as necessary.

Learning about assertiveness is easy. Doing it is hard. It takes mettle and it takes bottle. Doing it well entails girding any loins at your disposal. Put simply, it means putting your foot down, but without stamping. The word 'no' features strongly in the assertive vocabulary, but so do the skills of listening and negotiating.

Getting the assertive script right isn't that difficult. What is hard is looking the biz as you do so. A lot of people sound assertive but look like doormats. Others strive for flexibility and fairness, but end up looking like Dirty Harry suffering from mood swings.

Here are some bodytalk signals that show you are going too far towards either aggressiveness or passivity:

Aggressive Signals

▶ staring

▶ finger-pointing

▶ tight lips

▶ a stretched smile

▶ narrowed eyes

▶ standing too close to someone

▶ leaning over another person or their desk

- a sarcastic smile
- frowning
- folded arms
- looking away
- 'dead' eyes
- raised chin
- hands on hips
- hands behind head, feet on desk
- pacing
- making a fist
- nodding to interrupt
- an erect posture
- chest stuck out.

Passive Signals

- arms folded in a body hug or any other barrier gesture
- fiddling
- over-smiling
- a nervous laugh
- reduced eye contact
- hands rubbing face or playing with hair
- lowered chin
- a slumped posture
- drooped shoulders
- swaying
- shifting weight from one foot to the other

- hands stuffed into pockets
- hand-wringing or clasping
- sighing.

These are the bodytalk signals of an assertive person:

Assertive Signals

- even eye contact, used more when listening than speaking
- a smile that is reflected in the eyes
- no barrier gestures
- open gestures
- gestures used to add emphasis to speech
- listening signals employed
- nodding to encourage another person to speak
- an evenly-balanced posture.

These should help you to appear assertive – which may be half the battle in the end.

▶ How to Create Empathy

Expressing empathy and rapport is one of the best bodytalk stunts I can teach you. The technique is simple to describe and effective if you do it well. 'Doing it well' entails two criteria, though: i) subtlety and ii) guile. When you employ this technique you must never be sussed. Watch my lips: nobody must ever know you are doing this.

Mirroring is the name of the game and you've probably heard something about it already. Think of people you have rapport with already – your partner, your best friend, a colleague you work in tandem with. That rapport will be visible to outsiders. When you know someone well and like them you start to talk the same and move in the same way. Sometimes you even begin to dress alike. When you meet, your facial expressions will become similar. So rapport and empathy look like a mirror image.

In business we have to create instant rapport, rather than the long-term, grow-into-it stuff that is a by-product of friendship. Business relationships with customers can show all the signs of a relationship between friends, only without the socialising. This can be a hard act to pull off. You may only see the person a couple of times a year, yet you need to bond quickly. Client–supplier friendships aren't necessarily fake, but they aren't founded on all the usual values of friendship. There is a level of professionalism present.

Your job may be even more front-line. You may need to bond faster to a client than chewing gum to the sole of a shoe. This person will be a stranger both before and after the transaction. So mirroring is the ideal way to manufacture high-impact, effective rapport without being smarmy.

Fortunately, a moment can be all it takes to check out the customer's gestures, body posture, tone of voice and general demeanour and mirror it in a very subtle way.

I keep repeating the word 'subtle' for good reason. Some people with the brain of a newt will read this book and believe that the secret of getting on with others is to copy their every move like a mime artist doing the old 'invisible mirror' routine. This is not so. I have been on the receiving end of this sort of clumsy copying and it would be laughable if it weren't so ghastly.

There are various ways in which you can keep your mirroring subtle. If the other person is quietly spoken, you could drop the tone of your own voice. If they use barrier gestures, be less open with your own. If their tone is formal, keep to the same. If they are relaxed and friendly, reciprocate. That's all. If they scratch their nose, *don't* scratch yours. You can sit or stand in a similar position, but don't go over the top.

Leading

If you become good at this you can take it one stage further. If you are dealing with someone who is too quiet or nervous or closed or reserved, you can 'lead' them to relax and open up more by slowly adjusting your own signals.

The way to do it is to start in a similar position and gradually move towards a more relaxed or open pose. The person may take this as a subconscious 'lead' to relax their own behaviour. It's a bit like the non-verbal equivalent of small-talk to break the ice at a business meeting, or the small joke that dissolves the tension at an interview – a subtle invitation to calm down or relax a bit.

Key Points in a Nutshell

▸ Work can mean constant conflict between 'being' and 'doing'. The ideal blend is to 'be' perfect at your job and 'do' all the things that will signal your wonderfulness to all around.

▸ Improve your job skills if need be, but never underestimate the power of personal selling.

▸ Use the tips in this chapter to avoid falling into negative career traps, like stereotyping or negative mistake-handling.

Chapter 7

Specific Spatial Skills

I N BUSINESS, SPACE really matters, as we've already established. We all have our boundaries and territory. Now it's time to look at spatial skills in greater detail.

▶ Marking Your Territory

Look around at the space you work in. If you sit at a desk, you can see the finite boundaries, which is where your desk ends. If you are a teacher or lecturer, shop assistant or receptionist, the same will probably be true. Most jobs involve the use of a desk or table and a seat.

If your job involves a less defined territory, then you will have to think a bit harder. Wherever you work, though, you will have your own space. Even people who move in a world inhabited by others, like photographers, gardeners, or estate agents, will tend to have a work base to return to, maybe a darkroom or shed. Even if your office worships at the altar of hot-desking, you will have 'ownership' of a certain piece of territory for the period of time that you are using it. It may not be known generally as 'your' desk, but while you are at it any attempt to usurp it will still be seen as an act of aggression.

As already mentioned, we are nesting animals and will suffer from a lifelong urge to adopt small areas of space and then protect them ferociously. We start by marking out our territory. If your office allows open season on desk furniture, you probably work in a riot of personalised bits and pieces. Even hot-deskers will mark their territory. They hang a garment over the back of the chair. They 'forget' to throw coffee cups away, so that there are always at least a couple standing guard all day. They may not be allowed desk ornaments, but they have pens and other bits of officeware that signal sole ownership.

Territory can be marked by any object or piece of paper that has somehow found its way onto your desk. I have seen the usual furry animals, pottery pen holders, dying pot-plants, ageing post-cards, executive stress-busters, awards and photos of the kids. But I have also seen a plastic vibrator, two teaspoons taped to the PC frame, a row of dancing sunflowers, cacti, worry-beads and an oversize bra acting as headphones.

The floor-space beneath the desk tends to be even more anarchic in its accumulation of territorial clutter. This is often a true no-go area for other colleagues, who know better than to approach the 12 pairs of ancient trainers, two old plastic sand-wich cartons and five carrier bags holding God-knows-what that lurk down there in the gloaming.

If you were secretly filmed from above you would see the current scope of your infinite territory. Unlike the finite boundaries defined by the edge of your desk or counter, the infinite stuff tends to exist mainly in your subconscious. And yet its limits can be as defined as if they were made from barbed wire. So, you will tend to move in a particular space. If your chair is on castors, you will only trundle it within certain limits. Of course you will have to move through other areas, but your body language will change subtly when you do. Out of your zone you will become slightly more formal and social. Back in your invisible nest you tend to act in a much more secure and less 'watched' manner, even though others in an open-plan office can still see you clearly.

The same 'visible but invisible' behaviour affects us in cars. Drivers tend to act as though no one can see them. They rant and sing and pick their noses at traffic lights just as happily as if they were sitting in a screened-off area.

This probably accounts for the serial nose-pickers and crotch-adjusters in the workplace. Something about the nest psychology tends to make people think they are invisible to the naked eye once they are sitting at their desk. If your serial crotch-adjuster is happy to tout his trade in public work areas too, though, you are working with a complete anti-social pervert who either has no sense of bodily awareness or who is an avid exhibitionist.

▶ Space Bandits

It is important to recognise territorial ownership of both finite and infinite space. If we take the desk as the norm, your boundaries might be seen as extending to the edge of the desk. People leaning on, over, squatting on or placing things on this territory will be seen as 'space bandits'. Imagine taking one quite small and perfectly nice desk calendar and asking a nearby colleague if you can keep it on their desk. What do you think the response would be, even if there was room?

Professional space bandits are rarely that obvious, but their erosion tactics are just as horrifying. They operate in three different ways:

1. Sound banditry – polluting your ear space with their hyena-like laughter, mobile phones and Walkmans.

2. Air banditry – polluting your air space with the smell of their pot noodles.

3. Inch banditry – actually stealing real space from your territory. They start on communal or previously unclaimed space and work outwards, dumping paperwork or files or equipment there when no one is looking. They might also indulge in small acts of terrorism, like sitting on your chair or your desk, leaning across your desk or placing things on your desk on a temporary but hugely traumatising basis.

I watched one sufferer who had to cope with a carrier bag of food left unexpectedly by her chair by a space bandit colleague during a trip to the coffee machine. She became increasingly desperate in her bid to be rid of the offending article. When the colleague eventually claimed it in an exaggeratedly laid-back style, the woman had to pretend she thought it could be a bomb.

'But you can see the contents from here,' the SB told the entire office, adding to her humiliation. 'It's only a sandwich and a packet of crisps.'

That SB was breaking every rule in the territorial rights handbook. He deserved to have his tuna melt sandwich kicked from the fourth-floor window.

Beware of inadvertently becoming a space bandit. Standing behind colleagues, reading over their shoulder while they work, will feel threatening. So will leaning into the wrong territory or pulling round a chair until you have no barriers between you and are close enough to touch with any part of your body. Share-reading a document or brochure can be inhibiting. Allow colleagues and clients their natural space. Also allow them freedom of movement without request. We hate being cramped in any way. Yet we are usually too polite to ask someone to move back into their own territory.

▶ How to Protect Your Territory

The question is, how to hang on to your existing territory at work or even extend it?

How do you currently mark your own territory? What personal touches do you use? If you work in a shop or restaurant, you often claim territory by touch. Do you move items about before you start work? Do you dust or adjust things? Do you find yourself moving hangers on the rail, even though they are already straight? Do you find you have an urge to do this in front of the customer?

What you are doing when you make these minuscule adjustments is displaying ownership. In a way it is a signal that even you are there to serve, you are still the boss. Remember playing tag when you were a kid? How when you touched another child they then became 'it'? This style of touch to signal possession, ownership or 'passing on' is still very much part of both the mating/dating ritual and the work experience. You 'touch' a chair in a pub or restaurant by placing a coat or newspaper on it. You 'touch' a colleague's desk by putting a hand or a bag, coffee cup or personal work items on it.

Apart from touching, you can stretch your way into someone else's space. Watch the small power rituals that can go on all day if two colleagues share either side of a workstation and their legs can be stretched out into the other's space beneath the desk.

Rule number one about office territory: what you fail to claim, someone else will. So mark out your territory. Before you litter your desk with an array of toys and success-symbols, though, please remember that each item you choose says a lot about you in terms of image. As a quick rule of thumb:

▶ cuddly toys – 'I'm a cute little fun-bunny' or 'Look how desirable I am. These are all gifts from admirers who think I am cutsie-wutsie.'

▶ old post-it stickers – 'I get so few communications I have to save these that are past their sell-by date' or 'I need reminding about everything. I even forgot to rip up these old post-it reminders.'

▶ cards or postcards – 'I have few friends, otherwise why would I boast about the ones who have written to me?'

▶ photos – 'See – I may act as though I'm from another planet, but here is my family to prove I am humanoid.'

▶ executive toys – 'I am a very sad person' (saying you did not buy them yourself is no excuse).

▶ cacti – 'Go away and leave me alone.'

▶ bonsai – 'I like clipping things down to size.'

▶ funny slogans – 'I have no real sense of humour, otherwise why would I find this amusing every day for six years?'

▶ meaningful slogans – 'I like to imply I have depth and intellect. The reality is I got this little piece of wisdom out of a Christmas cracker.'

Once you have your desk sorted out, you can turn your attention to the rest of your territory:

▶ Use all your space. Put things in empty bits. Pace round it occasionally. Flex and stretch your limbs to redefine boundaries. Place stuff on the edges of your desk. Be as big as the space you own, in terms of movement.

▶ When you can, edge stuff away from walls and corners. Walls are good, because they make you feel secure if your back is to them, but never end up with your chair pressed against a wall or corner and your desk virtually right up to your chest. Reclaim land a little at a time, if you have to. Work late and move furniture inch by inch when everyone has gone.

▶ If your company allows plants from home, buy a nice one and place it in a spot a distance away from your desk. Pick somewhere that needs brightening and that no one else is using. This ploy will make that spot part of your unofficial space. It gives you an excuse to look across the room. The span in between you and the plant will then begin to become part of your infinite area.

▶ Never make yourself smaller in your own space. There's no need to employ arrogant 'spreading' gestures, but avoid any mouse-like tendencies. Never sit crouched or with arms and legs crossed.

The same should apply to communal areas where you are given temporary ownership, for instance, on a training course or at a meeting. Hanging your coat up in another part of the room is an excellent way of increasing your territory. Put papers out on your section of the table. Adjust the chair, if possible. Put down your own pen. Look around. Store bigger cases up the back of the room, if you can. Walk over and look out of the window while you're waiting for the course/meeting to start. Help yourself to coffee or water. Throw something in the bin. All the above can be done in an 'innocent' and relatively subtle way that should flex the power muscles without causing offence.

You can go too far, though. I once walked into my training room to find a delegate had arrived first and set up his entire office there. He had his laptop plugged in and glowing, his brief-case emptied across the table and he was busy on his mobile phone. When I walked in he was too busy to reply to my greeting and I felt as though I was going to be waved to a chair and asked to wait in my own room.

Shake Your Way to Success

One of the nicest ways of being territorial is a good greeting. 'Pressing the flesh' raises your profile while breaking the ice and also extending your space. When you present your business card your territory expands a little more. That card is part of you, but it will find a place in your associate's pocket, briefcase or even litter bin.

Smoking Space

Smoking has virtually been banned from the workplace alto-gether, although there are some companies in the furthest reaches of the Empire who still allot a smoking room, so that employees can puff away without recourse to Chapstick and a Pac-a-mac, in case of inclement weather down the park.

In terms of body language, smoking does, unfortunately, look quite cool and there is nothing quite like a ciggie as a prop to make you look as though you are lost in thought. Perhaps it has something to do with the tilted angle of the head and the narrowing of the eyes required to keep from choking.

If you do indulge, there is only one acutely negative body language aspect to remember: don't light up outside the company entrance. Smoking rooms are one thing if you want to gossip and scorch your lungs at the same time, but gathering in groups in the main entrance turns your entire building into something that resembles a soup-kitchen in 1930s' America. All you need is a brazier and the picture is complete. It makes both you and the company look ghastly. If you must ruin the view, go and smoke outside the building of a rival firm instead.

Toilet Behaviour

And while we're on the subject of unspeakable actions, smoking in the loo is out in terms of image-enhancement. Ditto eating. Or stopping to have a proper chat.

Toilets are useful at work for three reasons:

1. The obvious.

2. To do running image repairs, like tight or sock-changing, teeth-cleaning or deodorant-renewing, or hair-rearranging.

3. To be alone when an overflow of emotion kicks in. Where else could you take those sudden attacks of temper or tears, or stand by the sink with your wrists marinating in cold water while you wait for the blushing to die down?

Be wary of a colleague's privacy if they have locked themselves in a cubicle. They may have an OD of bile or blub to work out and are best left alone.

Lift Behaviour

Lifts demand a whole new style of body language, because they break all the existing rules. You are too close to strangers, some-times even touching. You are often surrounded by mirrors, making glancing around dangerous. You may know the people you are riding with – they may even be clients – but small-talk is difficult because of the small amount of time involved.

When you walk into a lift, always turn to face the door, unless you are riding with a very close work colleague. Otherwise your body language could be intimidating. As already mentioned, it is usual to watch the doors or the floor numbers as you ride – do not use eye contact as your proximity will render it threatening. Briefly acknowledge the other passengers with a quick nod or a slight smile. Only talk if you have accompanied the person you are with or if you know the other passengers.

Be polite: motion the other passengers out with your arm, especially if they are clients.

Thinking Space

I have included the act of thinking at work here because it is a very spatial skill, with many bodytalk complications.

Thinking is a good work skill – agreed? Staff need to be encouraged to think more. And yet it is something you are probably not allowed to do. It looks like skiving. It resembles day-dreaming. So most of the thinking at work tends to get done by the people with access to time, space and privacy. This will usually just mean the boss.

To think really well and be creative the brain needs to function in the alpha state, which is half-asleep, half-awake. It needs the following ingredients:

▶ calm

▶ time

▶ lack of external stimulation, like noise and distractions

▶ lack of pressure.

Fine. So you can just go and sit up on the roof for a few hours.

You probably also need some space. Cramped conditions do not enhance the creative process. If you work from home you will know what I mean. You stare into space a lot. You file your nails. You spend a long time gazing into the fridge and then eating nothing. You doze off on the settee. You also pace about quite a lot. Perhaps you even go for a walk to kick-start the brain. I need a café coffee and a browse through a tabloid.

Whatever your circumstances, try to spend some time thinking at the start of each working day. Either arrive at the office early and do it when no one is there or do it in the café round the corner.

If you need to do it during the working day you will need to acquire some bodytalk signals, especially if you work in an open-plan office or in another place where privacy is at a premium:

▶ Fold your arms with your fingers placed over your mouth and stare at the ceiling. Tap your fingers against your lips now and again.

▶ Rest your elbow on a chair and your forehead against your fingertips.

▶ Rest both your elbows on a chair and rotate gently back and forward with your lips pursed.

▶ With your elbow on a chair, sit with your face cupped by your hand to just below your nose, staring to your left at the floor.

▶ With your elbows on a chair, sit slumped with your legs stretched out, pencil tapping against your teeth.

▶ Talk to yourself (risky, but effective).

▶ Go for small walks, but try to look as though you have a mission. Carry documents. Stairwells can be good thinking places, especially in a tall building where everyone uses the lift.

Key Points in a Nutshell

▶ Be aware of your territory at work and the effect it can have on your perceived status. Give nothing away. Make use of every inch.

▶ Expand your empire. Claim any spare territory and extend your own via movement, greeting and legitimate deposits of personal business items.

▶ Watch your behaviour in certain communal areas, like the smoking room, lift or toilet.

▶ Spend some time each day just thinking.

PART 2

'Eye Listening': Reading Other People's Bodytalk

Chapter 8

Developing Your Basic Body Reading Skills

READING OTHER PEOPLE'S body language signals is a risky business. In fact it should come with a government health warning. Unfortunate types who don't get out very often may pore over Seventies-style body language illustrations of girls doing pelvic thrusts at drinks parties or men smiling knowingly with their thumbs tucked into their belt-loops, pointing at their crotches, but it's not that simple. Humans are subtle in their non-verbal signalling. It's this complexity that makes the whole subject of communication so fascinating.

Like your own outgoing messages, the people you will be observing will work with cluster signals, using a range of gestures and changes of expression from a dramatic sweep of the arm to the slightest eyebrow twitch. Some of these signals will be conflicting. Your boss may smile while telling you what you have done wrong or your best client could be frowning in disagreement while their hands are in pacifying mode. Remember that humans mask their own bodytalk signals. At work people may mask as much as 80 to 90 per cent of the time, because they want to create an appropriate impression, keep their jobs, be a good role-model for others, be liked or even emulate someone else.

So, to read others well you will need to be alert and you will need to keep an open mind. Assumption or lazy assessment of the more obvious signals will form a recipe for disaster. Initially you will need to be highly observant and to analyse the smallest detail. After a while, though, you can hopefully allow your subconscious to start to do the main graft again, reverting to a more learned and informed version of the 'gut reaction'.

You will also need to read others according to their values, not yours. We tend to see the world purely through our own eyes, assuming our opinions and decisions are right. However, we will take it that you are going to study others' bodytalk in an unbiased way, bearing in mind that they will react to situations in a different way from you because they think and feel differently. They have been brought up in a different place and they have worked with different role-models and stereotypes.

Finally, when you analyse others' reactions there is always one piece of the jigsaw missing – you. Other people will always be responding to your constantly changing image. Keep that knowledge at the forefront of your mind when you try to work out what makes them tick.

▶ Bodytalk Clichés

Business clichés are those hackneyed phrases that people use to hide their real feelings and thoughts. They are the lowest form of expression, a verbal ritual that says little because it says the same as everyone else, for example, 'Have a nice day' or 'We'll touch base on that one.' I don't need to go on, you'll have got the picture by now.

Body language has a whole raft of business clichés too. Like the verbal ones, these are 'masking' or 'delaying the message' gestures that either conceal our more non-professional signals or provide a routine solution to otherwise tricky moments.

Bodytalk clichés can be fleeting or they can form part of a longer routine. When you spot a bodytalk cliché in a colleague or client there is little you can do, apart from weather the storm. Like the wearing of a smart tie or lace-up shoes, they are part of the business performance.

Too many clichés will become boring, because they will leave you feeling hungry for a sighting of the real person behind the act. I have met at least two people who have become nearly total clichés and – strange to relate – neither of them is in politics. Long term, the effect is one-dimensional. You almost find yourself trying to peer around the back of these people's heads to see where the batteries are kept.

If you are going to keep that open mind we were talking about, you might decide that the 'real' person is too nervous or shy to come out and play. Unfortunately, faced with a smokescreen, we will often think the worst of what is being covered up. We fear the smile masks dislike or aggression, or that the baton-like nod of agreement is a sign that they really think we're talking utter rubbish. When it comes to mind-reading others, we are all true paranoids.

Expect the Best

I want you to learn to be a reverse paranoid instead. Believing others are thinking well of you is always the best wheeze, because it enables you to respond positively and optimistically. This in itself can be self-fulfilling. Don't beat me up on this one, though. There is a school of thought that says, 'Smile and the world will smile back.' I think that is partway bilge. There are people out there who resemble gargoyles and all the grinning in the world will never tease anything more promising than a scowl out of them. In fact, smiling at them can even make them worse, because they dislike you for being happy.

Pretend that we all begin from roughly the same starting-grid, though. The positive response will usually give you the best chance of a good outcome. When you come across masking and bodytalk clichés, don't automatically assume the person hates you. At least, not yet.

▶ Social Masking for Sanity

Social masking isn't really a sign of lying. Certain body language rituals, like a greeting smile, are an important part of business.

They make our standard behaviour more acceptable. Most of us have a side to our personalities that would be unacceptable in the workplace. It is irritable, bored, nervous, upset, unsure, childish, angry, hating, shy, panicky, dithery, confused – any or all of the above.

So people at work who refuse to mask in an attempt to 'be honest' are anti-social. Their behaviour is often disruptive to the team. If you work with a colleague who lets it all hang out emotionally you'll find yourself begging for a little polite concealment. 'Take me as you find me' is a statement of arrogance and disregard for others' feelings. People who operate like this may be easier for you to read, of course, but are a lot more difficult to work with.

▶ Analytical Processing

I'm going to ask you to do the impossible now. I'm going to ask you to be logical and analytical about a process you consider random. I want you to take several meetings and communications with other people and work out why you responded as you did.

First impressions are best for this, but you can analyse more ongoing interactions as well. I want you to examine all the messages you thought you were sent. Look beyond the words. How did you 'feel' each person was reacting?

Exercise

Plan three meetings that you are going to have in your working week. If you can, pick one communication that will be with someone you are meeting for the first time, like a new client or visitor. The second should be with someone you see occasionally, like a supplier or member of staff you have infrequent dealings with, and the third should be with someone at work you know well.

Go about each transaction as normal, but be slightly more attuned to the other person's messages and apparent feelings as you do so, plus your own responses and assumptions.

Think consciously about what is usually subconscious. Differentiate between what each person *told* you verbally and what you took on board from their non-verbal signals.

For instance, you may come to the conclusion that one of the people you saw seemed nervous. Think back. Did they *tell* you this or did you read it in some other way? If so, how?

After each transaction, write notes on the entire communication, listing the message you received or assumed, and how it appeared to have been sent. Start to look for any incongruence. You may have listed 'pleased to see me' as one signal and 'appeared to wish they were somewhere else' as another that underlay the first. Did they tell you they were pleased to see you while looking away and fiddling with their tie?

Turn gut reaction into statement of fact. Imagine you are in a court of law and are being asked to deliver specifics, rather than assumptions.

Creating this log of non-verbal signals will help you understand your own subconscious analyses. Once you have listed more of the stimuli, you can begin to arrange them into different headings. Itemise them under the following:

1. Overall posture and angle of body
(Erect? Slumped? Evenly-balanced? Leaning forward?)

2. Emphatic hand or foot gestures
(Arms folded? Legs crossed? Using a fist? Wringing hands?)

3. Emphatic facial expressions
(Eye contact, smiling, frowning, etc.)

4. Spatial play
(How they moved around and what space they employed during your conversation, i.e. did they become a space bandit or did they decrease their personal territory? How close did they get to you?)

5. Leakage
(Smaller gestures that appeared less intentional, like foot-tapping, jewellery-fiddling, etc.)

6. Micro-gestures
(Small, fleeting expressions or eye or blink movements that tend to be quickly masked.)

7. Denial gestures
(Those momentary insights into their opposing views.)

Ask yourself three further questions:

1. What was my overall impression of their mood/thoughts?

Then the inevitable and tough question:

2. Why did I think that?

And:

3. How much did their bodytalk reflect my own? At what point did my own movement affect theirs?

The third section of this book is going to deal with bodytalk dialogues and intentional or unintentional dialogues. Now is a good time to begin to monitor them, though.

When two or more people are in communication there is always a 'ripple effect'. After a while most of our non-verbal signals are responses to all the other action going on. This can cause massive fluctuations in our normal behaviour. For example, a colleague may have all the normal swagger of John Wayne, walking big and talking tough through his gestures and spatial banditry. Placed in a meeting with a Margaret Thatcher bossy-boots type, though, the John Wayne may respond by becoming Mr Bean.

Watching business bodytalk showdowns is often good fun, especially when the gladiators involved are involved in subliminal 'body-battles'.

▶ Fair Play

Assume you are never going to be a complete red-hot ace at reading others' bodytalk signals. Remember that it is not a precise science. I am a bodytalk expert and I would never presume to be blatantly authoritative about anyone's non-verbal signals, except as a party piece, when I am probably 80 per cent right, which means 20 per cent wrong. We are all sometimes so far off the mark that it is criminal. This is a subject where arrogant, know-all experts are an utter liability. So remember to be fair-minded as you make your assessments.

A recent TV programme showed a team of climbers searching for the remains of 1920s' mountaineer George Mallory on Mount Everest. They found a body on the mountain, but was it Mallory and had he been on the way up or on the way down? Had he completed the climb? The name tag in the jumper was that of the mountaineer. The discovery of goggles in his pocket suggested he was on the way down, because he would have been wearing them facing the sun on the ascent. The assumption was that this *was* George Mallory's body and that he *had* been the first man to climb Everest.

Then it was suggested the jumper might have been borrowed by a fellow climber. The goggles in the pocket may have been a spare pair. The ones the corpse may have been wearing could have come off in the fall. Letters to Mallory were found in the corpse's pocket. But the team admitted that nothing was conclusive.

This is a similar route to the one you will be taking in processing information about other people. One problem the team had was that they *wanted* the body to be Mallory's and *wanted* to prove that he was the first to get to the top. It was an emotive search. Your own investigations will also be affected by emotion. You will often search harder for what you hope or expect to find.

One colleague asked me what it meant when a man ran a hand through his hair as he talked. I said it could be a sign that he was confused or bewildered about something. It could also mean he suffers from an itchy scalp. Perhaps he has nothing more meaningful on his mind than an imminent bout of dandruff. But the woman fancied the man and wanted this gesture to mean that he fancied her too. She was massaging and bending the signal to fit her own ideal scenario faster than Uri Geller bends spoons.

▷ Cognitive Blindness

Apart from the wish-list factor, there is also the problem of 'turning a blind eye' to the messages that we most fear. This is another way of bending the visual evidence to avoid hearing an outcome that is unpleasant for us. It is often the reason why we believe the liar, even when we are able to read all the signals of evasive behaviour.

How often have you listened objectively to a friend's story about their partner's behaviour? You would place a large bet that your friend is being lied to. You find it hard to believe they can be so stupid. But you can see they are going with the stories. The smell of perfume on the shirt got there when he helped an old lady across the road – an old girl who happens to wear Opium. The lacy bra in the jacket pocket was placed there by a work-mate trying to get him into trouble. The hotel receipt with 'double breakfast' on it was a mistake made by the receptionist. Of course.

By and large, if we want to believe a lie, we will. When we are emotionally involved, every fibre of our being may be pointing us in the direction of the danger signals, but we will have developed myopia.

So, only search for the truth if you want to know it. If you intend bending the information to suit your desired version of events, you may as well not bother listening in the first place.

▶ Manipulation

Often people in the workplace will ask manipulative questions, both with their words and their bodytalk. Take the following scenarios:

Scenario 1

A trainer is running a course with a small group of managers. After she makes each point she turns to the group and asks: 'OK?' As she does so she raises her eyebrows, widens her eyes and nods towards each delegate. Her other question is: 'Does that make sense?', accompanied by the same series of gestures, this time even more exaggerated.

The audience all nod agreement every time. She then continues to the next point, confident that they are following her every step. But when the feedback forms arrive the next day, several of them have written that they were confused or had difficulty keeping up.

Scenario 2

A group of people are sitting in a restaurant, eating a meal. As they finish their last course the waiter breezes up, looking quite busy. 'Everything alright?' he asks the group as a whole, meeting nobody's eye. His chin is lifted and he is smiling confidently. His torso is turned away from the group, as though to continue to the next table. The diners nod their affirmation and a couple even mention the meal was great. Yet a complaint arrives a few days later, asking for a refund because the food was below standard.

Scenario 3

A couple are in bed together after having sex. The man lies back happily, smiling as he lights a cigarette. He then quizzes the woman: 'Was that good for you?'
  'Great.'
  'Honestly?'
  'Of course.'
  'How good?'
  'Wonderful.'
  'The best?'
  'Yes.'
  'Sure?'
  'Yes.'
  A few weeks later he overhears her confiding in a girlfriend that sex with him is like watching paint dry.

Each of those scenarios involved verbal and visual bullying. Of course it wasn't overt, but both the verbal and body language employed would have ensured a dishonest response. Given the choice of agree or disagree, be tactful or honest, most people will opt for the former, as it avoids conflict, quarrels and time spent on explanations. The delegates probably wanted the trainer to get on with things. The diners wanted to get away from the table. The woman didn't want a whole evening of soul-searching. It was easier to use mirroring, copying the trainer's nodding technique, the waiter's smile and the partner's pose of complete satisfaction.

You can barely stop yourself being manipulative with your bodytalk. There is no way to prevent others responding to your presence and the minute you meet with someone else you begin a choreographed two-step. Active manipulation is avoidable, though, particularly in situations like the examples with the waiter and the trainer, where it would have been useful for both to have heard complaints first-hand. (The guy in bed is debatable. Honesty would probably have deflated his ailing libido for good.)

The trainer should have been studying her delegates' body language for signs of confusion. When people drop behind, they stop taking notes, start frowning, employ face-touching gestures and end up yawning or looking away. Arms begin to fold. Doodling is rife. They could have been addressed individually or questioned on the last point.

The waiter should have employed the road-crossing technique: stop, look and listen. He should have shown he had time to listen to the reply. He could have used eye contact as he waited for the answer. His expression should have been one of interest and concern.

The guy in bed could have turned to face his partner and asked if there was anything else that she'd enjoy.

Again, keep an open mind when you read your visual feedback, though, because its only value will lie in your reading the signals honestly. Eye listening is pointless otherwise.

▶ Crowd-pleasers

OK, so perhaps there will be the odd occasion when manipulation can be appropriate. The main reason will be to sway the rest of the group or crowd in your favour. The trainer's objective will have been to educate, so crowd-pleasing would not have been a valid technique. But what about that political rally or after-dinner speech? Great speakers will often use techniques to arouse the crowd and increase general approval. There are tricks you can use with the tone of your voice or your gestures to ensure a round of applause or laughter.

Large groups suffer from herd mentality. When a few laugh or clap they all laugh or clap. Then everyone goes away thinking they had a jolly good time. Crowds create their own momentum. Sometimes they even enjoy themselves more when there is no performance at all. So swinging the large group can work if your main objective is to fool a lot of the people a lot of the time. If your aim is instant approval with loads of applause, then go for it. If you're looking to build a genuine relationship with your customers, then don't.

Key Points in a Nutshell

▸ Always keep an open mind when you read another's bodytalk.

▸ Work on any manipulative behaviour you may be employing – never try to massage a message into becoming the one you want to hear.

Chapter 9

Common Poses, Postures and Signals

HOW CAN YOU begin to get under another person's skin? How do you scrape away the business masking and manipulation and outright lying and start to see the real person hiding underneath?

The Visual Pause

Observing other people without appearing to stare is difficult. So how can you take more information in without causing offence?

Fortunately, reading bodytalk doesn't need to take longer than a few glancing seconds. As you learn you will need more time to assess and assimilate, but the eye will work quickly once you've learnt the techniques. Your current assessment rates run at a few meagre seconds. All you will be doing is using the same process, only with more knowledge and hopefully more accuracy.

I find it useful to observe through peripheral vision. Sometimes I barely look at all, to give me a chance to work with all the communications: words, tone and non-verbal. By flicking from one to another and occasionally turning off the visuals to concentrate on the vocal tone and words you will begin to work through every aspect of the bodytalk signalling.

Body-watching in business is much more 'socially acceptable' than outside the workplace. Work provides unique opportunities to stare without causing offence. You will become part of the audience when a colleague is speaking during a presentation, or less formally at a business meeting. You can happily observe every visual clue at an interview and you can study the dynamics in an open-plan office with all the intensity of a zoologist studying animal behaviour.

▶ Congruence

Your assessment of the visual clues will begin with congruence. When you watch someone speak or listen, you have to ask yourself if the messages they are sending out appear to add up. People are rarely congruent in all their communicated signals.

For instance, a financial director briefing an audience of shareholders would be pushing their luck and the audience's credibility to combine the following communications:

'We have suffered a bad year with below-expected annual turnover.'
(Wide smile, eyes fixed on audience, Winnie-the Pooh tie round neck, arms waving extravagantly.)

'But we expect to be looking at better trading figures in the next quarter, owing to reawakened customer interest in products and a renewed marketing campaign.'
(Looking down, rubbing back of neck, shaking head and sighing.)

You are horribly incongruent yourself a lot of the time. You've probably been guilty of smiling broadly while saying, 'Oh, I'm terribly sorry,' or telling a colleague who has interrupted you, 'That's OK, go on,' while thumbing through documents or tapping at your keyboard.

On the following pages are some posture/gesture/expression combinations that may provide a few more clues.

Standing

▶ **Feet more than shoulder-width apart, arms folded**
This pose implies a sense of confrontation. The person is spreading their centre of gravity as though preparing for a fight. The legs show a desire to assert their authority by spreading the territory. This person may want to be in charge, but in an aggressive, rather than high-status way. The folded arms imply a closed mind. *See drawing 1, overleaf*

▶ **Feet together, hands joined in front**
This is usually accompanied by a low-energy slumping of the upper torso. Feet that are together will imply a slightly prissy, perfectionist nature. This person may not appear pushy, but may be passive-aggressive, stubbornly fighting their corner in a quiet way. *See drawing 2, overleaf*

▶ **Feet one step apart, hands held loosely in front**
This person is displaying an open-minded, confident attitude and appears happy enough to do business with you. This is rarely the pose of the buyer, though. Sellers tend to be more likely to adopt this one. *See drawing 3, overleaf*

▶ **Hands on hips**
See this as potentially aggressive. The body is being bulked by this movement, which can be confrontational, especially if the feet appear 'planted'. If there is some bounce from the feet the pose is more likely to be the 'scout master' variety, suggesting leadership and authority, but with a jolly 'let's go and have fun' spin. *See drawing 4, overleaf*

▶ **Legs crossed at ankle, hands joined in front**
This balance-defying, gawky, coltish pose places the user in a precarious position. One move and wobble may set in. The main desire here is to mime helplessness and weakness. This person wants you to be non-critical and like them, possibly even help them out. *See drawing 5, page 136*

Standing

Feet more than shoulder-width apart.

Feet together, hands joined.

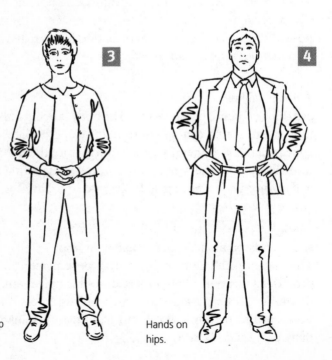

Feet one step apart.

Hands on hips.

▶ Legs straight, feet gone over at ankles

Very similar to the above, this 'little girl' routine is often a softener, sometimes from women in business who favour the balanced foot stride initially but who worry it may look too dominant and aggressive. *See drawing 6, overleaf*

▶ One leg straight, one bent in

This classic beauty queen pose is either adopted out of vanity or because this person has been standing for a long time and is changing the weight from one leg to the other in a bid to stop their back aching. *See drawing 7, overleaf*

▶ Hands clasped behind the back

Politely authoritative or even rather snobby. The hands have been de-employed here, which may be a politely passive move, as though the person wants to be seen as non-active and non-threatening. Hotel staff often use this position when in-between jobs, to signal 'not working but keen to help'.

The other reason behind this pose is completely different. It can look authoritative and high-status and imply 'I don't want to get my hands dirty on this one, so I'll keep them tucked out of the way.'

If the arm is being clasped, rather than the other hand, the person could be suppressing anger. *See drawing 8, overleaf*

▶ High-level hand clench

I call this one 'hamster hands' because it is so twee in a ghastly sort of way, resembling a hamster about to feed on a sunflower seed. I've only witnessed it from women and it is often accompanied by a girly voice. This person thinks acting like an ickle girly will make her look all helpless and loveable. Basically it sucks. *See drawing 9, page 137*

▶ The fig leaf

Men may pose as though appearing on a nudist beach for the first time, with hands clasped in front of their vitals. Obviously this is defensive. They are expecting criticism or disapproval. *See drawing 10, page 138*

Standing

Legs crossed
at ankles.

Ankles
turned over.

Beauty queen.

Hands clasped
behind back.

▶ 'Wedgie-hiking' or bottom-scratching
There is an obvious arrogance to either of these activities when performed in a group. Men do them often, women much more rarely. Whatever they mean, they need to be stopped.

▶ Talking or listening while the torso is turned slightly away
This displays either arrogance or nervousness. The person wants to avoid direct communication and is eager to flee, either because they think you are beneath them or because they are intimidated. Look for signals of either impatience or nervousness in other gestures. *See drawing 11, overleaf*

▶ Legs crossed while standing
Implies a person lacks confidence in what they are telling you.

▶ Leg bent at the ankle
Almost childish insecurity. Wants to be liked and judged favourably. Non-assertive.

Standing

9

Hamster hands.

Standing

Fig leaf.   Torso turned away.

Sitting

▶ **Legs crossed, arms open on the arms of the chair or loosely held in the lap**
Calm, relaxed and confident, or keen to give the appearance of such. *See drawing 1, opposite*

▶ **Perched on edge of seat**
The percher suffers from low self-esteem or guilt. Either they think their bottom is unworthy of the chair or they have been up to something and are keen to make a quick getaway. Watch one foot start to make for the door after a while. *See drawing 2, opposite*

▶ **Bags on lap**
Terribly nervous and insecure, this person is poised for quick flight or may even feel the bags form a castle wall between you.

Sitting

1

2

Legs crossed, arms
loosely held.

Perched on edge of seat.

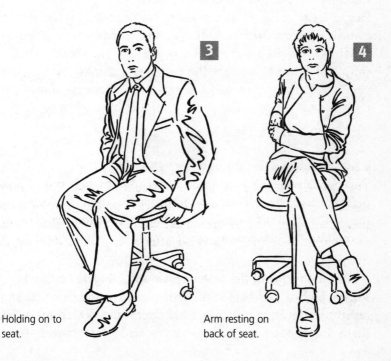

3

4

Holding on to
seat.

Arm resting on
back of seat.

▶ Holding on to seat

This rather childlike pose suggests a naturalness and honesty, but a lack of guile. There is obvious nervousness there, too. If they are short enough, their legs will start to swing after a while and then we are well back into kindergarten. If this person is reasonably confident this may be a ploy to look as though they are a child at heart and still retain a childish sense of fun. *See drawing 3, page 139*

▶ Arm resting on back of seat, hands lightly clasped

This pose appears quite demure and sophisticated. It is not as easy to pull off as it looks and this person probably spends quite a lot of time choreographing their movement. To succeed with this one you must know the height of the back of the chair and align it with your arm length and shoulder height, and you must get the elbow at the right angle to suggest laid-back relaxation. Also, the clothes have to be happy with the pose, or buttons will start to pull and bras or vests be exposed. *See drawing 4, page 139*

▶ Sitting on hands, or hands tucked between legs

Desperately retentive and possibly otherwise clumsy, this is someone who self-polices like crazy. Words will be chosen carefully. The person may even take elocution classes. After a couple of Bacardi Breezers the limbs will unfold, though, and you'll wish they were back in pin-down mode as things get broken and bashed about as they blunder around clumsily. *See drawing 5, opposite*

▶ Arm dangling down the back of the seat

This pose always looks laid-back to the point of inebriation. This person is a clumsy reactor who is a style-free zone. Lacking tact, they will mouth off happily, asking everyone around to 'take me as you find me'. *See drawing 6, opposite*

▶ Elbows on edge of the desk or chair arms, fingers steepled

This is high-status boss stuff. This person is judgemental and rather remote. Expect them to mask their responses like crazy. *See drawing 7, opposite*

Sitting

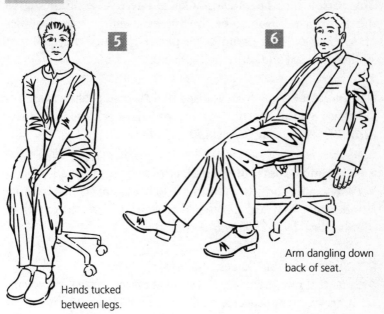

Hands tucked
between legs.

Arm dangling down
back of seat.

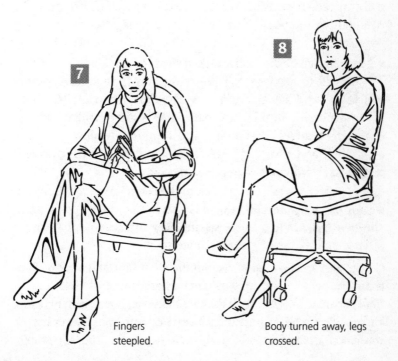

Fingers
steepled.

Body turned away, legs
crossed.

▶ **Arms folded on the desk under the chest, body leaning forward**
This person is co-operative and keen. There is very little side to them. If this is a woman her breasts may well be resting on her folded arms. There is no guile to this person, they are just straightforward and rather self-effacing.

▶ **Legs crossed away from you and body turned slightly away**
Whatever you did to this person, you have achieved complete turn-off. *See drawing 8, page 140*

▶ **Pulled into a corner of the seat, arms and legs folded**
Very defensive, possibly lacking in self-esteem. Unlikely to be co-operative. May feel threatened by you or fear confrontation. May be very shy. *See drawing 9, opposite*

▶ **Legs stretched out, knees wide apart**
Men do this one, especially in crowded places. They say it means nothing. Women suspect it is a form of phallic display. Either way it shows a disregard for social niceties. Expect this person to be competitive and possibly arrogant. *See drawing 10, opposite*

▶ **Legs crossed at the ankle, tucked towards the side**
This is said to be elegant. The person may have done the same course as I did at Lucie Clayton. The Queen favours this pose because crossing your legs from the knee is still considered vulgar in the right circles. This pose is also supposed to show your legs off to their best advantage, unless you are a man, in which case it just looks weird. *See drawing 11, opposite*

▶ **Legs tucked under the chair**
Shows a desire to hide away. *See drawing 12, opposite*

▶ **Legs and arms wrapped around the chair legs and back of the chair**
This person looks as though they are being held hostage. There just has to be a sense of insecurity here. Perhaps they always lost at musical chairs and intend to hold on to this seat as long as possible.

Sitting

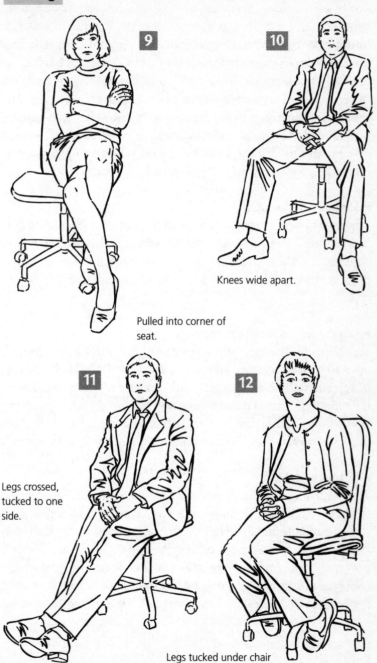

Pulled into corner of
seat.

Knees wide apart.

Legs crossed,
tucked to one
side.

Legs tucked under chair

▶ **Legs stretched out, arm extended across the back of the next seat**

I once saw a man sitting like this on the bus. It was OK until another man took the seat next to him. The normal thing to do would have been to have pulled the arm in and turned to face front. This man stayed where he was, an obvious space bandit of the highest order. The man next to him stood up to hunt for change in his pocket, obviously hoping the space bandit would do the right thing and pull the arm back. But no. After five minutes I concluded the space bandit must either be an alien, or foreign, or very, very mad. Then I saw he had his watch on upside-down. I feel that proved my point. *See drawing 13, opposite*

▶ **Slumped in the seat**

This used to be a power-pose in the days when the men at the top all had fat guts, wore waistcoats and smoked cigars. Now this type of pose suggests a lack of energy and commitment. If this person chooses to sit at the back they could be the troublemaker. *See drawing 14, opposite*

▶ **Leg crossed across the thigh**

This person is thinking about your proposal. Part of their mind is open to your suggestion and part is still closed off. There is a lack of agreement here, but possibly only because they are assimilating information. This is quite a high-status pose. If the leg is being held with one hand, the barrier is becoming more intense and the thoughts may be directly confrontational. *See drawing 15, opposite*

▶ **Sitting on a leg**

This person is capable of giving a job total focus. Still young and studenty at heart, they are reactive, rather than capable of considered action. Challenging when they want to be, they may also treat you to the 'shoes-off' or 'shoes-dangling' pose. If this is a woman you can also expect her to change hairstyles during a conversation, dragging one of those wretched scrunchies from her wrist to flick her hair into a ponytail. *See drawing 16, opposite*

Sitting

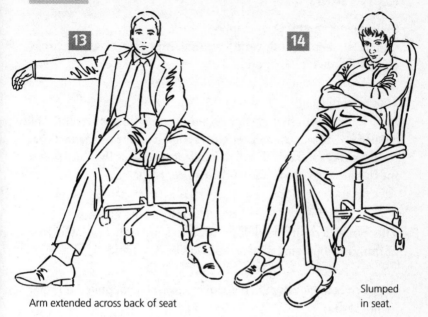

Arm extended across back of seat

Slumped
in seat.

Leg crossed
at thigh.

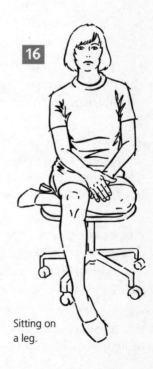

Sitting on
a leg.

Expressions

▶ **'Puckered' mouth or eyebrows**
Quizzical, considering your proposal. May even finger or stroke chin. *See drawing 1, opposite*

▶ **Suppressed smile**
A variety of options here, all meaning something different. The suppressed smile can register either a shared joke or the fact that the other person has a desire to laugh at you. In each of the poses, the lips are kept closed. *See drawing 2, opposite*

▶ **Lips closed, mouth pulled down slightly at the corners**
This can be a desire to look professional and only hint at a sense of humour following a joke. *See drawing 3, opposite*

▶ **Lips closed, mouth pulled down at corners, chin pulled up (the chin shrug)**
A speciality of Tony Blair's, signalling regret and seriousness. *See drawing 4, opposite*

▶ **Lips closed, mouth stretched wide horizontally**
This mirthless smile can appear threatening. It is a sarcastic smile, possibly denoting hurtful sarcasm. *See drawing 5, opposite*

▶ **Lips closed, one side of the mouth raised**
The sophisticated smile, intended to imply cool and intelligence. If it is aimed at you, the implication is that you are cool and intelligent as well. *See drawing 6, opposite*

▶ **Lips closed, both edges raised**
Strange and rather painful to perform, this is a forced hybrid and suggests bravery in the face of stress or tragedy. *See drawing 7, page 148*

▶ **Teeth showing**
More natural laughter and enjoyment *See drawing 8, page 148*

Expressions

1

2

Puckered mouth or eyebrows.

Suppressed smile.

3

4

Mouth pulled down at corners.

Chin shrug.

5

6

Mouth stretched wide.

Sophisticated smile.

▶ All the teeth showing

This is the stretched social smile, the sort you do when posing for a photograph. It is rarely genuine and either done to be ultra-pleasing or to mask intense anger and dislike. *See drawing 9, below*

▶ Teeth slightly apart, tongue protruding

Sexual. *See drawing 10, below*

Expressions

Bravery in the face of stress.

Teeth showing.

Stretched social smile.

Sexual.

Gestures

▶ **Arms folded evenly, no body pressure**
Relaxed listening. *See drawing 1, overleaf*

▶ **Arms folded in a 'body-hug'**
This indicates a need for reassurance. The person is feeling isolated and may have totally switched off from your message. *See drawing 2, overleaf*

▶ **Arms folded either high on the chest or with the hands in fists**
Conflict, non-receptive. *See drawing 3, overleaf*

▶ **Arms folded, hands clutching forearms**
Controversy. Set opinions. It will be difficult to gain agreement with this person. *See drawing 4, overleaf*

▶ **Arms held away from the body, spread openly, palms turned up or facing in**
This person is absolving themselves from blame or trying to achieve buy in from their listener via an 'empty embrace' gesture. *See drawing 5, page 151*

▶ **The above, teamed with a shoulder-shrug**
Denial. This person is trying too hard to convince and could be dishonest. *See drawing 6, page 151*

▶ **Hands on hips**
Confidence, high-status posturing, aggression. *See drawing 7, page 151*

Gestures

Arms folded evenly.

Body hug.

Arms folded high on chest.

Clutching forearms.

Gestures

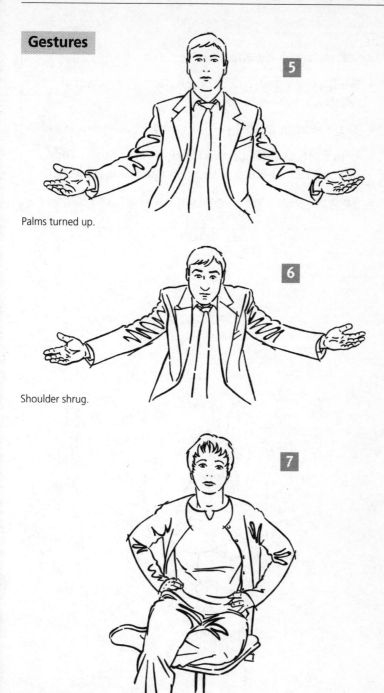

Palms turned up.

Shoulder shrug.

Hands on hips.

Key Points in a Nutshell

- ▶ Study others' bodytalk to become more proficient at reading it, but avoid staring.

- ▶ Learn to analyse what you currently see as 'gut reaction'.

- ▶ Watch others' facial expressions, posture changes and gestures to monitor their feelings and mood changes.

- ▶ Keep an open mind – never claim 100 per cent accuracy.

Chapter 10

*S*tudying the Armoury: The Props We Use and What They Mean

I N OUR BID to signal and communicate we will, like any good actor, grasp at props to help us make the point. Selection may be random, but at work there are usually a few items on hand to help us do what actors call 'a bit of business'.

Bad actors love props because they provide a diversion. In business, whether we use them consciously or not – and *not* is probably the most common conclusion – we use them to keep ourselves occupied when we're beginning to feel under pressure or stress. Paperclips, for example, are rewarding little objects to fiddle with and Blu-Tack can be used as dough, to remind you of the calm pointlessness of the plasticine class at junior school.

In fact a lot of this business has been learned in childhood. When the going gets tough, babies learn to suck their thumbs or stroke a cot blanket to create comfort and relaxation. A sales-person suddenly shoving their thumb into their mouth during a pitch for business would probably send out signals that all was not well. So they will opt for sucking the felt-tip pen instead.

A brief run-down on the silent language of props:

Pen Behaviour

In the workplace, the pen is far more than a tool for writing. It can be a comfort toy or a weapon. It is the thing we are most likely to be clutching most of the time. In a way, a pen has become the modern equivalent of a sword. The way someone uses their pen can give useful clues about their state of mind:

▶ Doodling – part distraction, part memory-jogger. When we doodle we are playing with our own thoughts, rather than listening to someone else. Doodling is like a 'fade-out' button on a hi-fi. You still hear what is being said to you, but you use the repetitive and unimportant movement as a way of tuning it out slightly. Doodling can be a sign that a person is preparing the appropriate words to make a point. Often the doodling will increase in speed or tension as they build up steam to speak. Or it could be that they want to speak up but are afraid to and are using the doodling as an outlet instead.

It can be useful to look at the patterns a doodler is drawing. Repetitive circles will imply a lack of conflict, but possibly a need for clarification. Angular diagrams can show inner anger that will often build in drawn peaks. Genuine, completed sketches or cartoons mean the doodler is lacking stimulation from your speech. You have been consigned to the level of background noise.

On a good day the doodler will be using the act as a method of aiding concentration. On a bad day you should beware, as the doodler can be the character who says nothing negative during your speech but who criticises you later.

▶ Tapping a pen on a table or paper, tip directly down – impatience, possibly building aggression. If this gesture is employed while the tapper is speaking, it can be acting like a metronome to emphasise their words. Consider yourself reprimanded.

▶ Holding a pen like a dinner knife and tapping it on a table or paper – milder impatience, often with good humour. This person is more distracted than the point-down tapper, though. This is a drumming movement that may be an attempt to change the pace of the drummer's (or speaker's) thinking.

▶ Pen point going lightly backward and forward across desk or paper – a more distracted gesture from someone who is being careful with their words. This person may not be saying what they truly think. The gesture is also a bit of a 'soother', so the person could be trying to calm things down. Any increase in speed will imply conflict brewing.

▸ Tapping the side of a pen on the edge of a desk – disagreement and building conflict. This is borderline aggressive behaviour. The person will usually be staring at the pen as they tap.

▸ Screwing and unscrewing a pen top – this highly impractical gesture is likely to be a sign of unease. This person is distracted and possibly stressed. There is a hint of eternal optimism or curiosity, followed by disillusionment. They may be wanting to speak but changing their mind.

▸ Complete dismantling of a pen – worryingly distracted to the point of stupidity, this person is searching for toys to play with. Let them go out for a walk around the industrial park.

▸ Whirlybirds – playing helicopter blades by twirling the pen around on top of the knuckles or twirling the pen in between each finger like a baton indicates a short attention span. Possibly not very bright, this person is still off in the toy box during meetings and one-to-ones. This type of complex routine takes practice, too, suggesting this person gets bored a lot. They may tend to sit meetings out and the main feeling of achievement for them may come when they twirl and balance the pen well. Enough said.

▸ Pointing – pointing a pen at another person to punctuate is an act of open aggression. Once it starts to be employed in a stabbing movement the message is obvious.

▸ Air-tapping – waggling a pen at another person in an air-tapping movement is equally aggressive, as though practising for hitting them over the head.

▸ Conducting – using a pen as a wand or conductor's baton is a way of increasing a speaker's authority.

▸ Clutching a pen when speaking – using it as a comfort blanket.

▸ Pen tapping lightly against the lips or teeth – non-committal mulling something over.

▸ Pen-chewing – inner conflict or worry. Shoving something in your mouth in times of anxiety just has to be a return to baby-hood. There is a frustrated, destructive spin to this one, though.

▸ Orifice-cleaning – pens can be used to clean any and all the orifices, but mainly the ears. This disgusting habit is partly an anxiety/comfort gesture, but that really is no excuse. Grooming rituals can be a sign of physical attraction, but this is hugely unlikely in this case, as the groomer renders themselves completely unfanciable by the gesture.

Pen-in-ear rotations can also be a childish and unconscious attempt to wind the brain up and often accompany thinking.

▸ Pens lined up in top pocket – over-organised, utterly conventional.

▸ Pens in any other outside jacket pocket – scruffy, badly organised, unconcerned about own appearance, either very boffin-like or extremely stupid.

Files, Clipboards and Coffee Mugs

Many objects are used as 'conscious co-ordinators'. You carry them around to give yourself something to do with your hands. Mugs are very popular with Tony Blair and his set. He touted one when he went to talk about the birth of Leo and most of his staff seemed to be carrying one for press conferences and meetings during a recent TV programme about Alistair Campbell. The effect is probably supposed to be 'low-key and informal', the 'just doing my day job and, oh, hey, yes, I suppose I am Prime Minister, actually' look that Blair tends to excel in.

Mug or glass-clutching provides three useful services:

1. It employs hands that would otherwise be waving or fiddling.

2. It provides a barrier as you lift the mug up between yourself and an opponent.

3. Sipping the contents supplies stalling time.

Clipboards and paperwork attain a more sinister use when given to women at work, though. Boadicea would have been proud of the way we transform anything A4 size into a breast-plate. See a colleague do this and you can rightly assume they feel defensive.

Plastic and Paper

Sheets of paper make useful props because they have the added effect of making the user look busy. Speaker's notes are a good example of the 'teddy bear syndrome', i.e. they do the same job as a cuddly toy when you are under pressure. Many speakers forget to use their notes at all, in which case you can assume they are there purely to give succour.

Waving paper notes around will mean something else again. It looks impassioned and slightly vindictive. Someone who is waving their notes above head level is trying to look like a genius with a new idea.

There is also a 'quietly mad' image associated with paper. Some people are as destructive with it as beavers with a log. In an apparent frenzy of masked anxiety, they will shred paper, roll it into little balls, fold it into aeroplanes, create God knows what in the name of origami, clean nails or teeth with it and even rip it into small twists and eat it.

The same damage can be done to Styrofoam drinks cups. These will be chewed, broken down into ashtrays, turned upside-down and have holes poked in the base, nibbled into confetti and have designs indented into them with the fingernail. All this is disturbing.

Après-training Rubbish Collections

When I study the detritus left after training courses I wonder – and worry – about the mentality of the people who created it. Every human emotion is recorded there, from anxiety to panic to fear. It is as though the delegates have ripped their souls from their bodies and pinned them to the desks. One day I will take three of the desks and sell them as art to the Tate Modern for a vast mountain of dosh.

I once hit on the cracking wheeze of sneaking around the desks during one of the breaks and thereby discovering all the inner workings of the delegates' minds so that I could modify my training tactics accordingly. This turned out to be a huge mistake. Trying to work with a manager who looks pretty normal but who you know has been squirrelling his sweetie-wrappers away in a large stash beneath his name-card is disturbing to say the least.

Clothing

People at work just love to use their clothing as props. John Major created perhaps the ultimate device when he began a keynote speech by taking off his jacket and casting it to one side. The signal was received loud and clear: 'I'm going to cut through the rubbish here.'

For most people, though, the prospect of performing an allegorical striptease in the workplace is remote. Consequently you will see many smaller uses for items of clothing, all of which can and will be revealing in some way or another:

▶ Playing with cuffs

This shows a desire to hide, i.e. disappear up your own sleeve, plus a need to look well-mannered and polite. Cuffs do need the occasional tug to stay below the jacket sleeve, but this natural spot of grooming has become a nervous, barrier-creating tic. This affliction rarely affects the lower orders, who may have no truck with devices like double cuffs and cufflinks.

▶ Checking the flies

This is an obvious sign of anxiety and insecurity and can be mistaken for what Billy Connolly calls 'checking your willy', which is more likely to be a sign of macho arrogance, plus a desire for childlike reassurance and comfort. Fly-checking can afflict both male and female members of staff and is usually executed just outside – rather than inside – the toilet door. The checking gesture will increase before business presentations. 'Always check your flies' *is* one of the most useful tips a speaker can be given, however it needs an extra clause: 'Don't do it in front of your audience.' I saw one presenter check his flies six times in quick succession as he started to speak. This is a sign of the anxious obsessive, the sort of person who will have to check the kettle's off about 20 times before leaving home.

▶ Buttons

Button-fiddling is similar to fly-checking because it shows anxiety and a desire to check and recheck. Gary Shandling built this gesture into the start of his routine as chat-show host Larry Sanders. When he began his stand-up routine he touched his jacket buttons several times. The gesture was so convincing it was hard to tell whether he was acting with his body language or not, which must have been very frustrating if it was a brilliant piece of 'business' that he had perfected.

▶ Neckwear

Ties provide acres of busy work for idle hands. Tie-straightening is a sure sign of defensiveness or nerves, especially if the person is wearing an open-neck shirt. Dabbing food stains off the tie with a finger will signify boredom to the point of near-death. Fiddling with the end of the tie will also hint at a distracted mind, although we all know that a man's tie is a phallic object, so heaven knows what sitting playing with the pointed end can mean. A woman fiddling with a neck-scarf can only mean one thing: she has tied the thing wrongly in the first place. No self-respecting business-woman would ever walk around with a bit of limp fabric dangling aimlessly.

▶ Tissues and hankies

Tissues are used as a prop more often than hankies and women have to be among the main culprits. Clutching a paper tissue in one hand shows nervousness and anxiety. The action renders the thing useless as anything other than a prop, as it will become a sodden ball within minutes. These props can be used at all times, though. I have worked with a woman who managed to type, telephone and even give business presentations with a hankie concealed inside the palm of one hand.

▶ The sock-plucker

I have only ever met one of these, thank goodness. When the pressure was on at meetings he would cross one leg over the other, with the ankle at thigh-level, and start to pluck at the wool of his socks. This was mesmeric and a little like watching someone plucking a chicken.

Key Points in a Nutshell

- ▶ Business people will often grab props to help their gestures along.

- ▶ Their choice of prop and manner in which it is used can give fascinating insights into their state of mind. Study and learn.

---

Chapter 11

*D*anger Signals: How to Tell When Something is Going Wrong

I T IS ALWAYS useful to know when something is going wrong in some way and you may need to change your behaviour to compensate. How can you tell when you may not be getting your message across or when you are dealing with someone who is angry, confused, disturbed or deliberately lying to you?

▶ Ways to Tell If Someone is Lying

Most business people are liars. Total honesty would be unwork-able. Lies come in layered form. Even in the 'honest' company, integrity may apply to big issues, like pricing, negotiating and staff communications, but there may still be those minor lies, like claiming a job is 'no problem' when it means disruption or smiling at clients when they are behaving badly.

Some business people are adept, grade-A liars, 'liar-savants', knowingly dishonest people who set out to pull the wool over your eyes. These people have often made a study of lying techniques and become good at them. They can be salespeople, politicians or chief executives, or in a variety of other jobs.

Then there are the 'honest rogues', the ones who lie, but in a way to let you know they are lying. These are the street-market style scammers, the sort who tell you a set of cheap crockery is Royal Doulton. You mind less, because you are in on the scam.

There is no foolproof way to spot the liar. Liars often give themselves away with time, though. Even the good ones find it difficult to perform without 'leaking' some signals:

Eyes

▶ excessive blinking – a sign of nervousness

▶ eye widening – a childish attempt to display 'What, me?' sincerity

▶ looking away – being furtive, not able to match eye contact because of guilt

▶ staring – an overblown attempt to avoid the previous syndrome

▶ more eye contact when talking than when listening – in natural communication it would usually be the other way round. This is a desperate effort to convince

▶ gaze moving to liar's top right – accessing creative part of brain

▶ one slow blink – often comes at the end of a difficult lie and is a cross between a self-congratulatory 'I think I got away with it' movement and a close-down 'Don't quiz me any more.'

▶ eyebrows raised – in mock surprise that anyone would distrust the liar.

Mouth

▶ the top lip becomes rigid while talking, almost as though the mouth muscles refuse to join in with the lie

▶ the lips pucker and purse in micro-gestures

▶ the mouth will be pulled down in a micro-gesture shrug of disgust or dismissal

▶ the smile stretches sideways, but fails to reach the eyes

▶ the smile remains fixed

- lips are licked
- there is a lot of swallowing or throat-clearing, as the person has a dry mouth.

Nose

- gets bigger – some research last year claimed that, like Pinocchio's, your nose actually increases in size when you lie. This was genuine research, but feel free to be dubious if you want. It's always nice to mock an academic now and again

- gets touched – nose-touching is a ghost from your childhood. Kids tend to cover their mouths when they lie in a gesture of guilt or expression-concealment. Grown-ups know this doesn't work past the age of 10. But we still like that little facial touch of reassurance while the lie pops out.

Head

- over-nodding in an attempt to gain agreement and approval
- forehead tilted forward
- the head tilted right down, chin into chest
- the body is kept still and movement confined to the head, which is held straight and rotates from side to side, like a gun-turret
- head tilted up towards the ceiling, trying to get away from the lie
- head movement in disagreement with words, i.e. nodding while saying 'no' or visa versa.

Skin

- sweats
- reddens
- becomes itchy.

Gestures

▶ the hands will either keep stock-still, like the rest of the body, for fear of the gestures looking unnatural, or will begin to over-gesticulate in a 'believe me I'm telling the truth here' kind of way. The hands held out to either side with the palms up and a shoulder-shrug is a classic of this genre, as is the hands held out in an 'empty embrace', which is an overblown bid to achieve buy-in.

The hands may also give signals that are at odds with the words, as when you are telling someone you love them while using dismissive gestures for example:

▶ fiddling – exaggerated comfort gestures, like playing with jewellery or clenching hands may suggest a need for reassurance when lying

▶ rubbing the back of the neck

▶ fingering the collar, literally as though it has become too tight

▶ rubbing an ear while looking down.

Feet

▶ shuffling

▶ tapping

▶ standing on the outside edge of the foot

▶ legs bound tightly together.

Breathing

▶ shorter, shallower breaths

▶ speech may be punctuated by a few deep breaths.

Remember that these are little more than clues, though, so you need to keep an open mind, even after spotting them. *All* of them can be innocuous, brought about by something trivial and unrelated to lying.

▶ Ways to Spot Discomfort

Discomfort could be a sign that your colleague or client is lying. It could also mean they dislike the topic of conversation or method of delivery. You could have touched a raw nerve or you may be using an inappropriate method of delivery. Perhaps you are intimidating your client by being too pushy or maybe your conversation has become too technical and gone over their head.

You may need to be aware of people's comfort levels purely for practical reasons. When I am running a training course or speaking at a conference I will usually be on the look-out for signs that my audience is too hot or too cold, or in need of a loo break.

Look for the obvious, because most people resort to quite overt signals when they feel discomfort:

- ▶ sudden barriering, i.e. crossing arms and/or legs

- ▶ swaying when standing or rocking when sitting

- ▶ pulling in the mouth, sucking in the lips but not puckering them

- ▶ glancing down at the floor

- ▶ hand-wringing

- ▶ nervously laughing or smiling when it is not appropriate

- ▶ rubbing or playing with fingernails

- ▶ scratching

- ▶ fiddling with clothes – straightening, buttoning and smoothing

- ▶ placing the hands between the legs

- ▶ stretching the mouth straight out to the sides with a display of clenched teeth

- ▶ sucking or chewing – anything, but mainly nails, fingers, hair, pens, etc.

- ▶ fingers resting lightly against lips

- literally squirming in the seat

- making repetitive gestures or actions

- touching the neck

- self-embrace gestures, like a self-hug

- glancing around, almost in search of escape

- rubbing the nose, touching the end of it or rubbing down the full length

- poking a finger in the ear

- rubbing the hands through the hair

- sighing.

▶ Attraction

This is not exactly 'how to know you've pulled', but a list of clues that the person you are dealing with likes you, primarily in a non-sexual way *(see also Chapter 19)*:

- eye contact that is more intense than normal, yet balanced with your own to feel comfortable

- a smile or change of body posture to something either more alert and straightened or relaxed when a person spots you – it's the contrast that counts

- a greeting that is just that bit more intimate than the normal formal one, i.e. a slightly longer hand clasp, a pat on the arm as you shake, more eye contact, closer-held heads or a less 'social' and more easy-looking smile that may turn into a laugh

- eye-softening – the whole area around the eye will appear to relax and soften in shape

- mirroring – as already mentioned, rapport between a couple usually means similarity in pose and gesture

- their torso pointed exclusively towards you

- the use of slightly but not overtly-familiar touches, like a very rapid and light touch on the arm or shoulders when guiding or steering

- a bending in towards you

- keen listening signals, eye contact, head tilt, nodding, etc

- gestures open and aimed towards you

- top leg in crossed-legs pose pointed in towards you.

▶ Conflict

This may be immediate, if a client has approached you with a complaint, or part of a more gradual build-up. With gradual build-up in a one-to-one situation you would look for:

- muscle tension increasing

- increasing alteration of pose, changing position in a seat more rapidly than with normal comfort needs or shifting weight between the feet when standing

- decrease of eye contact, sometimes until it is removed completely

- a wan smile with eyes looking down

- folded arms, increased use of barriers

- the head position going from forward-facing to slightly tilted back, i.e. chin lifting slightly

- the lips tightening

- jaw tension increasing, even to the point where speech patterns change

- dropped head, a hand running along the back of the head or neck

- pacing

- any leakage gesture that becomes more insistent, like increased tapping of fingers, fiddling with a ring, etc

- pen-tapping, point-down.

▶ Dislike

Conflict may be sudden and it may come and go, leaving friendship in its wake. Dislike is different, though. This may not emerge with the same signals as conflict, as it may be deeply buried beneath a mask of professionalism.

Business dislike has a long-suffering quality to it. It is something managers tend to pretend their team never suffers from, although dislike for bosses is a naturally-occurring phenomenon.

Most bosses nevertheless assume they are loved and popular, even though they are often getting people to do things they don't want to do. This assumption is a dangerous one. It may titillate the ego, but it leads to some pretty bad calls – like assuming staff are happy to work late and see less of their families because you are more important to them. As you can see, this is very flawed thinking that will only increase the 'dislike' factor and probably even encourage it to grow it into 'hate'. On the whole it would be better if bosses imagined that their workforce disliked them intensely and tried to work from there.

There are two reasons for their delusion:

1. Arrogance and a feeling of omnipotence.

2. The workforce are masking their dislike. In terms of reaping what you sow, they know the moment the boss starts to dislike them back is the day their job is doomed.

Boss-dislike can only be viewed in its naked state on the day the boss leaves the company. If you are a boss, remember one sobering fact: the higher the levels of smiling, celebrating and mawkish sentimentality at your leaving party, the more pleased your staff are to see you go. Watch their faces as they present you with that carriage clock. Would they really be grinning and cheering so much if they were sad to lose you?

Other signs of dislike may include:

- ▶ colleagues over-smiling at you

- ▶ people stopping speaking when you walk into a room

- ▶ no one making eye contact

- ▶ your neighbours building workstation barriers – they may angle their PC to block you off or place a line of desk paraphernalia between you

- ▶ barely-masked tension in people's hands when you communicate – watch for fists or fiddling gestures

- ▶ a lack of body commitment when you stop a colleague to talk. They will never turn face-on, except when the relationship turns to open conflict.

- ▶ colleagues sitting back in a seat with their hands behind their head and their feet on the desk when they talk to you

- ▶ colleagues leaving you to lurk at their desk when you want to talk to them, making you wait while they finish an important chore, like cleaning the plaque out of their keyboard with a paperclip.

The look you need to catch above all is the expression change once your communication is over. This is where the smile turns to a small grimace or pucker, the eyebrows raise or the eyes roll towards the ceiling in a look of exasperation. This is obviously hard to spot. The only way I can suggest is for you to use your peripheral vision. Finish a conversation and turn your gaze back to your work, but see whether you can catch anything out of the corner of your eye.

▶ Envy

Anyone who has achieved any measure of success in their lives will have encountered envy from colleagues or loved ones. Envy can hit anyone at any time and it stinks because it makes you feel so guilty. It is the taboo emotion. It is shameful and so it has to be masked.

For supreme envy-masking moments you only have to watch competitors in sporting or award ceremonies, or even beauty pageants, when the winner is announced. As the envy levels rise, so do the attempts at masking by the losers. The masking may even reach crisis-point and fall over into farce. The winner will look distraught, shake their head and cry – all of which would be far more appropriate behaviour for the losers. They, poor souls, are forced by convention to indulge in smiling, laughing, whoops and air-punches as they race to hug the very person they most dislike in the world at that moment.

Similar acts of bravery take place in business nearly every day. Envy at work is commonplace and may be created by promotion, company cars, better desks or offices or even a boss–employee relationship. Only very occasionally does an outbreak of honesty occur. I saw one employee who just couldn't cut it when the promotions were announced. He threw his pen down on to the desk and skulked off scowling. Others were shocked that he hadn't been big enough to join in the hop-across-your-desk-and-skip-up-to-bounce-around-the-winner ritual. I quite liked him. He badly wanted to win and let that show through for a moment.

▶ Confusion

This is not a hard one to spot, because people forget to mask it. Watch someone who is lost in a building. They will happily display their bewilderment in the hope that someone will spot their distress and offer them help.

Confusion at work generally looks like this:

▶ head-shaking

▶ pausing

▶ hands placed on the desk, palms-down

▶ fingers on lips

- face-touching
- face-rubbing, especially the forehead
- neck-scratching
- neck-rubbing or rubbing the hands through the hair
- frowning
- shuffling through things
- head tilted to one side
- lips pursed, often twisted to one side
- sitting back in a chair, arms folded, mouth closed and stretched horizontally, the corners of the mouth puckered into the teeth
- head suddenly dropping forward
- exaggerated signs of thinking: the body pulled back into the corner of the chair, arms folded, eyes raised reflectively to ceiling, eyes narrowed.

▶ Stress

Stress-spotting is a favourite pursuit for managers concerned for the well-being of either their staff or their company finances, in case of litigation. Spotting true negative stress can be a little like searching for a tree in a forest, though. We're all suffering stress these days and are often easily able to verbalise our discomfort. The more serious cases do tend to keep it to themselves, though. They become ashamed of their own feelings and worried others will think they can't cope. They will deny rather than boast about their stress-levels. Stress can create paranoia, which is why they try desperately to prove everything's OK.

That's why you might look for:

- raised shoulders – the muscles contract with the tension, making stress victims do a bad impression of Ted Heath
- shortness of breath – breathing becomes shorter and shallower

- ▶ trembling hands
- ▶ rapid movements
- ▶ sudden movements
- ▶ rushing around the workplace for no apparent reason
- ▶ frowning
- ▶ increased comfort gestures
- ▶ neck-touching
- ▶ forehead-rubbing
- ▶ exaggerated puffing, blowing air upward with the bottom lip pushed out, blowing air from the mouth up the nose
- ▶ a big intake of breath now and again
- ▶ lots of hand-clenching when talking
- ▶ arms placed across the stomach
- ▶ obsessive-looking fiddling – the sort when you want to reach across and physically stop the person from doing it
- ▶ making more noise when they work, banging things around and sighing
- ▶ an increased blink-rate
- ▶ decreased social smiling.

▶ Nervousness

Nerves are a shocking thing because we expend so much effort trying to mask them in work situations like interviews and presentations, where they are a perfectly natural by-product. The danger is that cover-ups achieve nothing more than a 'pinball effect', where a relaxed state of mind is over-exaggerated to the point where you start to look arrogant, stuck-up or impolite.

Spotting nervousness in others can help you because you will understand that it might account for their inappropriate behaviour. Signals include:

- an increased use of barrier gestures
- excuses for barrier-creating, like straightening the tie or clutching a bag
- throat-clearing
- an increased blink-rate
- exaggerated and increased swallowing
- lip-licking
- reassurance gestures – face and nose touching, hair smoothing or fiddling, playing with rings, rubbing knees
- increased smoking or sipping at a drink
- a smile that doesn't touch the eyes
- breathless speech
- giggling
- lack of co-ordination, clumsiness
- irrational facial ticks.

▶ Denial Gestures

We've mentioned these before. I love them. They are the afterburn signals, the add-ons, the ones we throw in to say that we were 'only joking', or 'didn't really mean it'. They can be the ultimate in rudeness or a sign of someone who is being heroically polite. They can be a symptom of wariness and a signal of honesty. They can accompany bouts of strenuous masking or can merely be a sign of low self-esteem and lack of confidence. You will see most of them if you hang around long enough to catch all the action, as best bits often come at the end of a communication, or at least the more honest bits do.

Denial gestures often come in micro-format, although we sometimes shout our message from the rooftops with big, semaphore-style gestures. A verbal version would be on the occasion of Prince Charles's engagement, when he was asked whether he and Diana were in love. 'Yes,' he replied, adding, 'whatever that means' before the nation barely had time to prepare a sigh of delight.

Now think of the same thing in visual terms. The classic denial tactic comes when someone is on the receiving end of a fulsome greeting. Men in particular tend to favour the social hug. This is a sign of empathy and affection for the other man, although, hang on a minute, mightn't that give the impression that the affection is something other than mere blokeish bonding? No problem. In a manoeuvre non-subtle enough to make your eyes water, the chaps will thump each other's backs furiously.

I watched a macho group of young men meeting up recently. You could tell by their faces that they were overjoyed to see one another, but then that was obviously deemed to give too much away. They started doing fake punching and thumping to even out the balance again.

This affection-and-retraction gesture is commonplace throughout our lives. A parent may hug a small child and then send it away with a pat on the bottom. As a kid, you could get a kiss on the cheek and a hair-rumple or be cuddled one minute and tossed up into the air the next.

Social interactions offer up the same double act. When a man makes a pass at a woman, she might fend him off by tickling or patting him, a subtle sign that she's not interested in him in that sort of way.

Even a business handshake can result in a denial gesture. One US businessman decided to give his counterpart in the UK a pretty fulsome and long-lasting two-handed shake. The UK guy went through an agony of suffering from this over-friendly (by UK standards) greeting. In the end he opted to pat the other guy rapidly on the forearm as a way of 'breaking' the clasp.

Spotting the denial gestures in these types of circumstances is vital in business, because these may be the only signals we get that we have overstepped the mark.

Constant Denials

Some gestures are virtually constant and if so, you need to ask yourself why the person is sending them out.

For instance, it is quite common in a business meeting for someone to try to convince the group that something is a good idea while happily sending out hand signals to the contrary. This contrast in signals is more than just incongruence. The victims may find themselves signalling the one message they desperately don't want to give out.

Perhaps total commitment scares us. Your speaker may be trying to get buy in from you, but offering you an alternative at the same time. This is almost a manoeuvre for embracing failure by offering it as an option.

Here are some of the reasons that may lie behind denial behaviour. Any or all of these may apply:

1. To be polite. Tension can become unbearable for people if they feel there is pressure on someone to be convinced by or in agreement with them. They stick a denial gesture in to break that tension and invite their listener to be honest in their response. They have made the request but are offering the option of refusal. By acting out a negative response, however fleetingly, they present it as a viable option.

2. It may be their response to a 'don't' command. They may have been telling themselves not to look nervous or harassed and this is their body's immediate response.

3. They may be genuinely unconvinced by their own argument or product or attempt at masking and, in the belief that they have given the game away anyway, try to show a more honest face so that they are not accused of being deceitful.

4. They may have found themselves in a physical situation that is worryingly inappropriate, like the fulsome handshake or the male body hug. The denial gesture is used as a counter to any potential charge from the other person, bystanders or even themselves that the thing got a bit intimate.

There is a wonderful scene in the film *Planes, Trains and*

Automobiles where John Candy and Steve Martin find themselves, as strangers, having to share a bed together. They wake up to find themselves accidentally snuggled up and spend the next few minutes punching one another, striking macho poses and talking about football in a bid to redress the balance.

Key Points in a Nutshell

▶ Be alert for negative body signals. You may need to change your behaviour.

▶ Never let ego stand in the way of receiving these signals. Ignoring them can be a mistake.

▶ Use them as warning signals. Plan ways of discussion or change based on what you see.

---

Chapter 12

*D*etecting and Dealing with Mood Changes

S O, JUST WHEN you think everything's going swimmingly, when the colleague, boss or client is chatting happily and seems to be thinking your way, there is a sudden discernible mood swing. You are frustrated and confused. What happened? Did you call them by the wrong name? Mention their dead mother? Inadvertently imply their husband sleeps with camels?

Good communication means being totally tuned in to these fluctuations in another's signals. Sometimes they are red herrings but often they will require a change of tactic on your behalf to get things flowing well again.

If you are the one doing the talking, now is the time to stop. You need to take stock. Find an excuse to get the other person talking so that you can be analytical. Ask them an open question. Listen and keep the conversation flowing in the direction they choose.

Now analyse what happened. At what point did the mood change? How did you read that change of mood? Did they stop doing something, like nodding agreement? Did they suddenly close down, did they employ more barriers? Did they turn away?

Look at their present positioning. What is it telling you? Look for four possible scenarios:

1. Disagreement and turn-off

They may have been displaying open body language, nodding agreement and smiling. Is their body now turned slightly away from you? Have they leant back in the chair? Have they crossed their legs away from you? All or any of these could be a sign of disagreement.

2. Frustration or anxiety caused by turn-off

Did they suddenly present more barriers? Did their arms fold? Did they cross their legs for the first time? Did you notice any face touching? Did they begin to 'comfort touch', fiddling with jewellery or clothing?

3. Impatience

Did their movements become more rapid? Did they change position in the chair? Did their nodding speed up? Did their top leg in a leg-cross start to swing? Did they glance at their watch? Appear distracted? Did they place their hands palm-down on the table or start shuffling their papers?

4. Boredom

Did they stifle a yawn or appear distracted? Did their posture slump? Did they start to employ mindless repetitive gestures, like doodling or rolling their pen around?

If you observe any of these clusters you need to take drastic action.

Your response in terms of bodytalk needs to be geared towards whichever of the signals you believe you are being sent. I would never recommend dramatic 'repair swings', where you try to salvage the situation by modifying your own signals in a desperate manner. Apart from anything else, remember that you may be on the receiving end of misleading gestures. When you see a change of position and start going through agonies of soul-searching, it could just be that their discomfort has been caused by their foot going to sleep, rather than acute boredom or rabid conflict. However, don't use this more optimistic version to lead you to ignore the signals. You need to take action, just in case.

Bear in mind that any listener will drift in and out of a conversation. We listen in loops, allowing the mind to go on small walkabouts. These loops can be of great use when you are selling. If you allow pauses after the main points, the listener will be able to trot off mentally for a few seconds, while they take in what you have said and apply it to their own circumstances or experiences. For instance, a salesman selling double glazing may pause after telling the potential buyer how great the new leaded windows would look with their stone-cladding and how jealous all the neighbours would be. The pause will allow the buyer to imagine Harry and Carole down the road catching sight of the new windows and clutching one another in uncontrollable envy.

Training, or implanting any important message into the brains of your audience, will warrant the same mental looping. The brain thinks at around 400–600 words per minute, while a speaker will talk at about 125 wpm. Some small walkabouts are inevitable, then.

What you don't want, though, are the sort of loops that last for a while. These will be the boredom loops. Listeners also roam when you have become too complicated for them or your jargon is unfathomable or they disagree with your basic premise and have realised that argument will be unproductive. Salespeople need to be especially tuned in to these signals, which is why there is more on this in Chapter 17.

Apparent boredom needs a change of tack. Move your own posture to create energy. Vary your tone a little. As soon as possible use a visual aid or get the listener speaking. Ask them a question. Get them involved. You are obviously rattling on too much, which is never good in any communication. Remember, nature gave us two ears and one mouth and we should use them in roughly that ratio.

If you sense impatience, it is also vital to take action as soon as possible. Some people have short attention spans and low boredom thresholds and you need to respect that, rather than fight it. I know this because I am one of those people myself. When you read impatience, then, you can start by beating yourself up. You have gone on too long. You failed to study your listener. By the time they are sending out these signals they are desperate, believe me. They have gone beyond being polite.

You need to provide instant reassurance that the end is in sight. Tell them you are on to your last point or that you only have a few more minutes of information left to cover. Stop and ask them their views. Put more energy into your body language. Check your watch and say you are keeping in mind the time of their next meeting, etc. Give them a light at the end of the tunnel. But never give them false hope, as then they may just lose the will to live, let alone the will to listen to what you are saying.

As for disagreement, if you sense this, there is little point battling on. Work your way though the point you are currently making and then stop the proceedings. Invent a way of getting your listener to voice their opinions. Even consider asking them if there is something they disagree with. Keep your body language relaxed and open. If you close up as well, or display conflict, or that you are hurt by their change of attitude, you will lose them altogether. Employ confidence and eye contact. Ask the question and then show open-minded listening skills as they give you the answer. They may even be blunt, but you must remember not to flinch. The worst technique is to invite criticism and then argue with or refute any that is given.

If you spot a more frustrated or anxious turn-off, you will need more subtle ways of getting to the root of the trouble. Either the person is a poor communicator or they have no great desire to tell you what is wrong. You need to drop your tone a little, pause and maybe rearrange your own papers to create a brief gap. You might throw a quizzical gaze in their direction, which would mean a tilted head, chin slightly down and eyebrows forming a raised frown, or a straight head, chin dropped low and both eyebrows raised. Both these expressions will provide an invitation to them to speak their mind.

When you listen to their point, lean forward slightly and place both arms on the table or chair-arms in an evenly-balanced gesture. Your facial expression can register concern, but never that you disagree.

▶ Group Situations

Talking to groups, say at a meeting or presentation, will mean you have to respond to herd fluctuations. You will receive mixed signals and your ideal response will be harder to gauge. One person may be gazing at you with rapt attention while another is looking out of the window, apparently pondering the meaning of life, the universe and everything. The main point to remember is to stay calm, keep reading the signals and don't over-react.

Puzzlement is often the easiest to read and dealing with it quickly will offset later, more acute symptoms like boredom and switch-off. Remember, the good thing about puzzlement is that people are often more than happy to ham it up like crazy when they're suffering from it. They will frown, touch their pen to their mouth and scratch or tilt their head.

If you spot a bewildered-looking listener, find out what the problem is. Use their name, but don't patronise or make them feel stupid. 'Would you like me backtrack on one of those points?' sounds a whole heap better than 'Was there something you didn't understand?'

I have witnessed 100 per cent group puzzlement and, believe me, it's not a pretty sight. One was when I was speaking to a large audience in Glasgow and they had a problem with my South London accent. It was about 10 minutes before they tuned in and then everything was OK. The other was when I was asked to be a guest speaker at a school in Harrow. I talked for about half an hour about self-motivation, wondering why they were looking so confused. It turned out the teacher had muddled the dates and told them they were getting a talk from the Tampax lady.

If you sense a group has gone beyond bewilderment into total turn-off, you have probably either used a term they don't understand or you are telling them something they have only just heard from another speaker. Trainers, for example, use games and exercises to illustrate their points. One trainer can follow another and unwittingly use exactly the same exercise. Audiences rarely point this out. When herd mentality kicks in they would rather sit and take time out than point out your *faux pas*.

Proof of this comes with one of the frequently-used tests of listening skills. The trainer throws several trick questions at the group to challenge their ability to listen. One of them is: 'How many animals at a time did Moses take into the ark?' The answer given is invariably: 'Two.' The idea is to then point out that it was Noah, not Moses, and that the audience was therefore not listening properly, ha, ha.

I now ask: 'How many of you heard that I said "Moses", not "Noah", and were too polite to correct me?' This will often turn out to be the majority of the group, who will then tell me they thought that I was simply in the first stages of early senility.

A Mixed Bag

So, what to do when the responses are more mixed?

The answer is that you should go for the negatives and handle them as you would verbal questions or challenges, while not relying on the positive responses, either. Personally, I find smiling nodders more spooky than the turned-off listeners. In my experience they are more likely to give bad feedback.

Pinpoint 'bored' before anything else because it usually elicits a strong visual response and also because it is more catching than herpes. One goes, they all go. Speak louder, pick up the pace, show a slide, bang on the flip chart, ask a question – just do *something* quickly to get them going, otherwise you'll find it's only you and the smiling nodder who are still awake.

Never ignore the less active members of the group. Screen-savers and other negative-looking types are probably just assimilating all the information you're throwing at them. Don't cut them off without a backward glance. Keep including them in your gaze and ask for their responses.

As for people who complain, remember they are not the enemy. Many of them are trying desperately to stay as your customer. Don't alienate them for disagreeing or being judgemental. Be their friend too. Keep them on board.

▶ Going for the Push

Perhaps the most dangerous signal to watch for, though, is the one that shows you have made someone feel they are being pushed. Persuading and influencing need to be subtle tools. When you reach the point where a person feels pushed you can consider yourself in trouble.

Think about it. What happens when you push? One minute you are in useful discussion and the next you are wielding the big stick. What do you think the other person's response is likely to be? That's right, they will start to resist or even push back. It's a natural reaction. Then the odds of you achieving agreement are remote. Pushing turns negotiation into argument.

If you are the boss, you may feel you have the right to push staff. In a way this is indisputably true. But do you really want a team of donkeys working for you? People who feel they have no right to an opinion? People who don't bother challenging or discussing anything because they know you will win every time? The point is, you won't win their agreement, just their silence. And if there is no negotiation involved the work gets done, but not very well.

So, be flexible and receptive in your approach. Don't end up in a push situation where resistance becomes more important than compromise. Believe me, I know what I'm talking about here. If I feel a push coming on I will hunker down, even if I agree with the basic proposition. Salespeople who suss this aspect of my character know they are handling the mother of all suckers. There was the estate agent who told me one house was out of my pocket, only to have me sprinting off to the building society to up the loan offer. Then there was the car salesman who told me I wanted 'a nice cheap little run-around to take me to the shops'. I had to buy a Mercedes Sport just to prove him wrong.

Saving the Situation

Let's say you have gone too far and have pushed. How will you read your blunder in the other person's bodytalk?

In general you will find yourself looking at two contrasting sets of signals. 'Push' will usually either mean shut-down or World War Three.

1. Shut-down

This is shown by hedgehog-style behaviour, including:

- folded arms
- dropped eye contact
- crossed legs
- a blank facial expression
- blushing
- cold-smiling (the mirthless variety that we do when put on the spot).

The main signal to watch for is the eyes. If the attention and interest has been genuine prior to the push, you may see a triangular action. The person's gaze will start on your face but swiftly drop to their bottom left and then scud across to their bottom right. This is the trapped look. The lips will often perform a small pursing movement to accompany it. Sometimes the eyes will come back to meet yours again, in which case it may well look like a flying circular movement.

This person is trying to escape, while at the same time accessing all the relevant parts of their brain to come up with an excuse. If they settle their gaze on their right-hand side they are telling you they are being forced into a lie to get out of the 'push' position.

2. World War Three

Straightforward hostility to the push will be all too easy to spot, even when the other person is making an attempt at masking. The signals are as follows:

- chin raised, maybe even stuck out
- staring
- tightening of the mouth
- spine-straightening
- head-shaking
- raised eyebrows

- a fleeting expression of disgust and naked anger that will be quickly masked, often by an amused smile

- a very brief flicker of cold hatred in the eyes that may then soften or be averted

- denial gestures – a throwaway hand movement, or raised hands implying 'So what?', a small nose-laugh, where air is expelled through the nostrils noisily while the eyes close in a slow blink, or a sucking in of air between the teeth

- hands on hips

- a sudden desire to stand

- attention much more focused in your direction

- a decrease in comfort gestures

- an increase in 'tension' gestures, such as repetitive movement

- turning the head slightly and looking through the side of the eyes

- frowning

- jaw tightening, teeth clamping together

- a smile stretching

- finger-waving

- chopping movements with hands

- actual fists.

Why not simulate this one in the comparative safety of your own home? With most family members it can easily be achieved with the word 'why', as in: '*Why* do you wear so much brown?' or '*Why* do you park the car like that?' Watch the body language response – the aggression and intense focus will be instant enough to be hilarious, while the verbal response is likely to be: 'What's wrong with it?' If you want to, you can continue the research by going into shut-down mode with the reply: 'Nothing.' The ensuing communication should provide ample opportunity to study cornered 'push' aggression first-hand before you meet it at work.

▶ Double-layering

All these mood swings and symptoms of concealed thoughts need careful and constant reading for business success. Speculating on the behaviour behind the behaviour has even become a favourite workplace sport.

The general thrust of this type of conversation will be: 'That man is a complete and utter bully. You should have heard how he spoke to Barry yesterday.'

'Yes, but I think a lot of it is bluff. I'm sure that he only shouts to hide his insecurity.'

A colleague of mine with a very high-status job was recently bemoaning the fact that the new MD had been treating her like a badly-behaved junior and humiliating her in front of the other staff. The man was obviously an ill-mannered bully but she added seriously: 'I know why he does it. He loathes public speaking, it scares him to death and it's my job to manage him at all the big conferences. Every time he sees me he is reminded of his fear and this makes him act aggressively.'

Her analysis told me what a fine person she was to look beyond the bluster. But so what? Does it really help to know or guess at the cause of bad behaviour?

In work situations it may not help the perpetrator, but I believe it can help the *victim* because it starts to remove the personal aspect of the conflict. This is part of the repair system that the mind uses to buffer the unbearable. We prefer people to treat us badly because they feel threatened by us or are jealous of us, rather than they dislike us. If we get turned down for promotion we like to decide that it was because we would be too good at the job and therefore threatening to the rest of the management team. We tend to play the same mind games with any failed relationship.

The other reason we like to scour the past for excuses is that when we do we find we are studying the child rather than the adult before us, or as Americans call it, 'the inner child'. It is always easier to tolerate bad behaviour from a naughty child than it is from an adult. Kids don't know any better. The very thought makes us feel grown-up and parental. It puts us on top of the situation. Never mind that the naughty kid is a 43-year-old adult with an £80,000 salary. Never mind that his job as a manager is to motivate and communicate and that he isn't doing either.

Frankly, though, I don't give a fig about the inner child when it comes to tailoring my response to bad behaviour in the work-place. What you need to question is not just the 'Why?' but the 'How?' *How* will you deal with it? How can you read it and then begin to turn the situation to your advantage?

That is really what the third section of this book is all about.

Key Points in a Nutshell

▶ Monitor body language signals from others and be alert for any changes.

▶ Be prepared to respond to changes. Analyse your own behaviour.

▶ Steer towards a more positive response.

PART 3

An Invitation to the Dance: Applying Body Language Skills in Specific Workplace Situations

Chapter 13

Meeting and Greeting

I N BUSINESS WE interact with what is often an extremely wide
section of people. So, meeting and greeting are potent skills in
your bodytalk repertoire. If you create a good first impression
you can afford to coast a little later on.

Some business relationships are so fleeting they never go
beyond this very first approach, which is an even stronger reason
for tackling the ritual and getting it right.

I am going to work through very specific workplace situations,
although most of them will be common to a variety of careers.
Many of the situations will be ones that you encounter on a daily
basis, but may never quite have mastered. I rarely encounter
people who can meet and greet well. Why are we so bad at the
commonplace? I believe there are four possible reasons:

1. Laziness
2. Fear
3. Arrogance
4. Stupidity

Take your pick – the choice is all yours.

The only one I will have any truck with is the second. Meeting
and greeting, dealing with clients face-to-face, business/social
events, presentations and sales meetings can all scare the pants off

us at one time or another – possibly all the time. There is no hiding-place with most of these situations. We are on show and we are being judged accordingly. We think we ought to be good and we are scared of the consequences when we aren't.

So, your first task will be to go back to the section on confidence and your bodytalk exercise *(see page 32)*. However you feel inside you are going to walk into each and every one of these situations like a warrior. No creeping, no dithering, no shilly-shallying about, OK? Treat everyone you meet in business as an equal. Be a reverse paranoid. Assume in advance that their response will be positive.

▶ Global Variables

It is easy to imagine that business cultures are global in definition, that while countries retain their traditional social customs, modern corporate life has created its own world-wide bodytalk etiquette. Nothing could be further from the truth and ignoring this simple fact causes misunderstanding and even offence on a regular basis.

Foreign business travel is a facet of working life. Expecting foreign visitors or hosts to both understand and even mimic your behaviour is arrogant. The best you can do is to judge what is the norm and try to follow suit. Bear in mind that even regional differences will apply. In London, for instance, it is becoming the norm to be fulsome in your greetings, especially in marketing and the media, where a hug or a kiss on the cheek is quite appropriate. Suggest this in the north of Britain, though, and a shudder of disapproval will normally go round the group.

The most important factor is to be aware of the potential for difference. If you are hosting foreign visitors do some research. Ditto if you are travelling abroad. Most companies are happy to give details of their country's way of meeting, greeting and doing business.

Foreign Bodytalk Cultures

The French will shake hands at the start and end of meetings, even with colleagues they know well. Gesticulation is the norm, although avoid overt displays that may make you look like a bad impression of Maurice Chevalier. Body posture is less formal than in some European countries.

Germans are similar in the greeting rituals. Colleagues will greet one another in the morning and evening and even when they meet for lunch. Their work demeanour is generally quite formal and eccentric behaviour is frowned on. They are charming in their approach, but expect inappropriate behaviour to be commented on. The British will tend to keep negative thoughts to themselves but Germans consider comment to be acceptable.

Italian business people tend to be open and communicative. Emphatic gestures are the norm, but so are the polite rituals like listening and affirming agreement or understanding. Eye contact is less reticent than in more northern European countries. There is great emphasis on being well-groomed and smartly dressed. When you are in Italy, your body language should reflect an aura of humour and positive thinking.

In the UK there is still an air of formality about business body language signals. Emotions are generally masked, although everyone is expected to use humour in presentations. Showing a sense of humour is to appear 'normal' and trustworthy. The handshake is used on formal greetings only. Colleagues will never shake hands during the working day if they have been working together. Apart from the handshake, most other touch is seen as inappropriate. Business cards will be produced at the end of a meeting and it is considered a little rude to read them studiedly in front of the giver. Gestures tend to be self-deprecating and anything that looks arrogant is disliked.

Greeks are natural face-to-face communicators. They are great and uninhibited users of expression and gesture and what may sound like a heated argument to UK ears may just be a mild negotiation. True turn-off for a Greek business person will come with silence and a more withdrawn demeanour.

Swedes share a tendency with Russians to 'under-respond' in

their listening language. Whereas British and Americans will employ nodding and changing facial expression to register full attention, and often find interruption appropriate, the Swedish will take it in turns to talk while the listeners sit in visual and verbal silence. Russians may be completely deadpan, which can be intimidating to more southern speakers.

Americans employ an aura of energy in their business bodytalk. Greetings may be quite fulsome and the handshake can go beyond the straightforward European 'two-hander' affair. A touch on the arm or the shoulder or a two-handed clutch can be considered appropriate, depending on the relationship being defined. Business cards are an important ritual and will emerge very early on in a mutual exchange.

The Japanese have a similar sense of ritual in their card exchange. Greetings will be formal and include bowing. Cards will be produced in both hands and should be received in the same style, before being studied. Polite body language is expected at all times. Emotional displays are seen as a sign of losing face and weakness.

Australian business bodytalk is polite but friendly. Greetings and handshakes are very similar to those used in the UK, but once the formalities are over there is more warmth and energy than in the British approach.

Gesture Signals

Each culture tends to acquire its own 'gesture shorthand' and it is vital that you remember the potential for global misinterpretation. Each country has its own 'insult gestures', for instance. In the US it will be 'the finger', where the middle finger is raised from the fist. In the UK it is the V-sign, although turned in the opposite direction, this will signal victory. Flicking your fingers along your chin from back to front is an insult in France and Italy.

▶ Making an Entrance

Present yourself well. Walk into any room as though you have a right to be there. But prepare yourself first:

▶ Take a moment This may sound unimportant, but it isn't.

▶ Pull up your posture. Do your posture workout.

▶ Breathe well. Expel all the tension and any underlying nerves with a long slow out-breath.

▶ Get rid of your screen-saver face. Create an expression that says 'charming and confident'.

▶ Transfer any bags to your left hand. Better to do it now, before you are confronted by the offer of a welcoming hand-shake.

▶ Check your grooming.

▶ Put an expression of lively intelligence into your eyes.

▶ Never walk in looking stressed or harassed.

▶ Be speedy, but never rush.

▶ Look pleased to see the person you are greeting.

▶ Study the door as you approach. How does it open or revolve? Doors are tricky. Many are made of glass, which makes a clumsy entrance something to be enjoyed by all the staff in reception. Think before you enter.

Once you've got this far, go for it. Sweep through the door with confidence and look pleased to be wherever you find yourself on the other side. Never creep into a room or squeeze through a barely-open door. What next?

▶ Practise the old finishing-school trick of closing the door behind you without turning around. Step in front, keep eye contact, step back and allow the door to close behind you. This is a great trick for charisma-buffs.

▶ Walk across to the person you are greeting looking pleasant and full of anticipation.

▶ If you are meeting someone in reception and are unsure who it is, ask the receptionist, but do it subtly. Don't point or go into a whispered huddle, followed by the turn-around-and-stare routine. Never stand in the middle of a crowded reception yelling out your guest's name.

▶ Name badges are difficult. They are a great aid for name-spotting, but you should never talk to someone while staring at their left breast in rapt attention.

▶ When you approach your visitor, smile, use eye contact, say their name and extend your right hand for the shake, which you – as the host – will instigate.

▶ If you are the guest, stand up as you see your host arrive.

▶ Give good warning of your intention to shake hands. Extend your hand from about five paces away. Never dither with the arm, waving it around as though unsure whether to shake or not. Dithering is contagious. The pair of you will be down trash alley in no time, dropping bags, laughing nervously and banging heads as you bend to retrieve stuff from the floor.

I once arrived at a company with a colleague in her car. The client was waiting outside to greet us. My colleague put a bag and some books on the car roof while she did up her coat. They slithered to the ground and I leapt across the bonnet, trying to save them. We spent a few minutes trying to repack the bag and when she was finally ready to walk towards the building, she opened her umbrella and poked me in the eye. By the time we got inside the client had caught our clumsiness and decided to join in the act by sliding over on the floor.

▶ Prepare for foreign visitors. They may not shake hands. Most will expect to, if they are in the host country, but there are always cultural and religious aspects to take into account. Study the culture beforehand and prepare your bow, if necessary.

▶ Once you have shaken hands, try not to go into the 'oily creep' pose, holding hands together at waist height or higher and bending slightly towards your visitor. Keep your arms to your sides and supply open gestures to steer your visitor towards the lift or office.

▶ Some cultures expect an exchange of business cards at the first moment of greeting. Have your own ready, just in case, and receive theirs confidently.

▶ If you are visiting a UK client, keep your cards with you until the end of the meeting. Handing them around at the start looks a bit flash for UK tastes. It smacks of the hard sell.

▶ Keep all your movements smooth and well co-ordinated. If you are greeting visitors in reception, walk the job beforehand. Check out the sequence of doors you will take them through and any problems with the lift doors (i.e. do they close quickly, can you hold them with an outstretched arm while you usher your visitor in, etc).

▶ It is more polite to greet important visitors in reception in person than to send a PA.

▶ If you are the visitor, watch your host and hope they are good at steering.

▶ Never peer into offices or stare while you are being taken around a company.

▶ Wait to be offered a seat when you arrive in the host's office.

▶ Never start unpacking the contents of your briefcase on the host's meeting table until your host has made some claim on the territory first, either by placing their own documents there, or by putting their arms or hands on the table.

▶ Always be good at offering refreshments to visitors. I recently visited one financial company where coffee turned up in a huge Styrofoam container with a tight-fitting plastic take-away lid. Getting the lid off without sloshing the contents everywhere was a nightmare. The drink was too big and too hot for the length of meeting. When you had drunk enough, you had nowhere else to place the lid and dirty beaker apart from back onto the desk of the guy who was interviewing. It felt as though you were using his desk as a waste bin.

▶ Get drinks ready rather than leaving your guest sitting by themselves in your office while you go to the coffee machine. That gives them the opportunity to have a sneaky rifle through your papers, too.

▶ Meeting and greeting means an exit handshake, too. Take visitors to the main entrance and formalise your farewells. Never do a good first impression, only to flunk the last one.

Key Points in a Nutshell

▶ Practise your entrances and exits.

▶ View your meetings and greetings as prime time, in terms of image.

▶ Perfect your approach to new visitors.

▶ Hone skills like shaking hands.

Chapter 14

Interview Techniques and Appraisals

ANY INTERVIEW IS important in career terms, but the recruitment or promotion interview is especially vital. Much is riding on both sides during this relatively quick and formal communication, so tension is often high. A lot depends on your personal impact. You are expected to speak well, both in verbal and visual terms. Interviewers read honesty and ability from posture, dress and gestures, either consciously or subconsciously.

Pre-interview work is vital. You need to know how you will come across and how you want to be perceived. Here are a few pointers:

▶ Planning should start weeks before the interview itself, when possible. Find out as much as you can about the company you are approaching and its culture. I have known many applicants who haven't really taken a look at the place until they're sitting in reception just prior to being interrogated. If possible go and take a look a few days beforehand.

▶ If you're having trouble deciding what to wear, choose a smart, well-groomed outfit that says nothing much at all and create your personality verbally. A dark-coloured simply-cut trouser suit should do the trick, even with a company that is more casual in its image.

▶ Beware mirroring a very casual look if that is what you observed on your first visit. Many companies have a 'dress-down Friday' policy. Turn up in chinos on a Thursday and you'll get laughed out of the place.

▶ Take a good business bag that is easy to handle. Keep it tidy inside and full of good pens and some businesslike paper for taking notes.

▶ Wear good shoes. Most companies get the heebie-jeebies at trainers or anything clumpy, but would even take on Son of Sam if he showed up wearing a well-polished business lace-up.

▶ Rehearse in your kit. Sit in front of a full-length mirror and go through the motions of being interviewed. See how your clothes move and what their limitations are. Does the skirt ride up? Do you flash flesh between sock and trouser hem? Sort it.

▶ Practise sitting well. You will need to look confident. Try your prime position and then work through a few variations. Pull yourself into the back of the seat, unless you are so short your feet miss the floor. Place your elbows onto the arms of the chair and fold your hands in your lap. Cross your legs.

This is a good prime position as it looks confident and comfortable and implies you are ready to listen. It also gives you scope to manoeuvre. Always place your business case down on the floor beside you. Never leave it with your coat, even if invited to do so. You will need to go scuttling back to retrieve pens and diaries.

▶ If you are straight from school or college no one will expect you to turn up fully tooled up like a Yuppie, with electronic organisers and a mobile phone. If the job is office-based, though, a business case is still a good idea. Otherwise go empty-handed or carry a handbag. Whatever the job, never walk in carrying a newspaper or any non-interview goodies.

▶ Leave yourself plenty of time to get there. Rushing is the enemy of laid-back and cool.

▶ Do your posture and preparation exercise *(see page 60)* before you walk in.

▶ Make a good entrance *(see page 193)* and keep making them as you are shown into offices and around the building.

▶ Carry bags in your left hand.

▶ Sit in the chair offered, but keep in mind you can move it a little. Interviews are a game of territory and high-status/low-status. If you are applying for a job it is important you observe the lower-status rules to a certain extent. This doesn't mean grovelling horribly, but it does mean no attempts at stealing the interviewer's space or invading their territory.

Moving the chair or altering its position too radically can be termed predatory and offensive behaviour. Be aware of your personal comfort zones, though. Moving within the correct space can have an effect on your feelings of well-being. If you are an interviewer, you should always try out the candidate's chair yourself first.

▶ Interviewing Positions

You may be interviewed from behind a desk, or there may be nothing between you and the interviewer. They may use a board table or a coffee table. Your seats may be formal or sofa-style. You might be interviewed by one person or a panel.

Layout 1: Face-to-face across a formal desk

This is the equivalent of the missionary position in sex. It is normal bog-standard fare. One more recent problem that can gum up the works is the addition of the PC to most desks, which can act as an extra barrier. Interviewers should ensure the thing is pushed well to one side. I had a recent meeting with one manager that involved us peering at each other over the top of the machine like two little meerkats.

Legend has it that this position is confrontational and that the desk acts as a barrier. I believe a lot of us prefer it because it is usually what we are expecting.

The desk does create a barrier but this acts as a safety screen for a nervous candidate. It is formal, but then so are most of the easiest interviews. It's the overly informal that can be more threatening. When the whole session becomes too chatty it's easy to forget what's at stake and drop your guard. This is great for the interviewer because it acts as a truth drug, but less helpful for the candidate.

At the start of the interview, the interviewer should come around the desk to shake the applicant's hand and offer them a seat. The applicant's chair should not be placed directly opposite – always angle it slightly and leave space between the chair and the desk.

If you are being interviewed, try to achieve this angle as you sit down. Make the gesture appear casual, but pull the back of the chair towards you and slightly to one side. Always avoid sitting right up to the desk. This 'dinner table' position is not appropriate in this type of situation. The interviewer can and probably will use the desk in this manner, placing their hands and elbows on it, but you should never follow suit. Keeping a space between your chair and the desk ensures you have room to move comfortably and that the interviewer can watch your body language.

Interviewers should avoid a desk position that halves the room. Most offices are oblong and a lot of desks are positioned right in the middle, almost like a centre line. This is probably the worst use of what may be quite a cramped space. Angle the desk so that the corner is behind you, rather than the straight wall. This looks less imposing and gives both you and the interviewee more room to relax in. Try it – it feels better.

Layout 2: Interviewer Sitting Angled Across the Corner of a Desk with the Applicant

This is usually done to be kind and thoughtful to the applicant, because it is less confrontational. It is very much the classic doctor/patient position and, yes, it is a whole lot less barriered and confrontational.

A lot of its success depends on the position of the desk, though. If it is pushed long-side against a wall it can feel natural. With the normal layout, it will appear contrived. Even against a wall you should ensure both parties are angled so that they have empty space behind them. I once sat in the corner-angle position with my chair against the wall and felt the interviewer was about to take my blood pressure.

Layout 3: 'Interrogation'

Here, the desk is all that stands between you and a panel of interviewers. This position is virtually unavoidable with group interviewing, but it does leave you feeling you are under interrogation. It is vital that the chairperson introduces each of the interviewing panel in turn and that you take any opportunity to shake them by the hand and give an individual greeting.

Your chair will need to be a little further back than with the one-to-one interview, as you will be rotating your attention around the group and will need more room to manoeuvre. Always look at the person who asks the question when they are talking and when you begin your answer, but then widen the scope of your gaze to include the entire group as you talk.

Layout 4: Across the Coffee Table

This is all a bit more low-slung and groovy and probably part of the 'Hey, let's just have a bit of a chat' style of interviewing. It has a set of problems all its own.

Low-slung seats can play hell with your business suit if you are dressed formally, especially if you are wearing a skirt. Think carefully before you sit down. How can you maintain your dignity?

The worst sofas are the deceptively soft ones. You dump yourself down, expecting a modicum of support, and find yourself sinking backward. Try not to issue the normal cry of 'Woah!' If you find yourself more slumped than you expected, comment from your Quasimodo pose on the wonderful comfort of the seats. Then pull yourself smoothly into a more upright position without doing an impression of an upturned stag beetle.

Trousers are a must here, as then you can sit middle-seat,

turned at an angle towards the interviewer, legs slightly apart and hands on lap. If you are long-limbed, you may even make it to the back of the seat.

Finally, remember that crossing your legs when sitting can be difficult if your bottom is lower than your knees.

Layout 5: Seat-to-seat

This is no hiding-place stuff, a chair-to-chair confrontation without any form of barrier. Although this position is often favoured by well-meaning interviewers with a short course in psychology beneath their belts, I find it appallingly uncomfortable. Think socially. Where do you have the best chats? Over the dinner table? Over coffee in a café? Would you invite a guest to your home and sit them facing you with feet nearly touching and nothing between you? I doubt it.

Before you meet this situation at work it would be wise to try it at home for a while first, just to get used to the feel. See how getting closer decreases your feeling of comfort. While you talk you will become aware of the potential for accidental foot-touch as you move your legs. Your movements become inhibited accordingly.

Pull your chair back until you have reinstated a feeling of security. This is your personal zone of comfort. Be aware of it and try to engineer it subtly if you are interviewed in this way. Crossing your legs may help, but avoid crossing your arms as well or your discomfort will be too obvious.

▶ Interview Tips

▶ Try to limit your own movements slightly at the start of the interview. The interviewer will be looking at you and working on first impressions. Like take-off and landing for a plane, the start and finish of an interview can be the most dangerous times. Sit well in the seat, engage in a little small-talk but be prepared to listen, rather than gush.

▶ Keep your laughter to a minimum. Nervous laughter is a killer. There's no need to be unsmiling, but avoid the over-ready guffaws.

▶ Accept a drink by all means, but think about the choreography if you are tense or nervous. When will you sip it? Will you interrupt your own speech to drink it or will you do it while the interviewer is talking? Can you do that without looking distracted? Can you carry on the eye contact and nodding over the brim of the cup?

▶ Start in your prime position, but keep in mind you will be mirroring as well in order to gain rapport. When you mirror at an interview, keep status in mind. Never look more relaxed than the interviewer and never be more casual in your approach. If the interviewer appears relaxed, you may tone your own pose down a little. If they look as though someone has shoved a broom handle up their back, then keep your own pose more formal. Many interviewers get nervous and you will only make them feel worse if you look terminally untroubled. If in doubt, err on the side of looking rather nervous. Interviewers expect this. It shows respect for the occasion.

▶ Keep your eye contact constant while listening and vary it slightly when talking. Avoid 'over-thinking' with your eyes, i.e. staring up at the ceiling for long periods of time. It is a good idea, however, to look away thoughtfully during the pause after they have asked a question and you have formed the answer. This gives the impression that the question was a good one and you are being honest in your answer. Total eye contact and a speedy answer look a bit too pat.

▶ Allow your facial expression to change while you are listening. Respond to what the interviewer is saying, but don't over-react or you will look phoney.

▶ Nod while you are listening.

▶ Keep your hands closed when you are listening and use them for emphatic gestures when you are speaking.

- Leaning forward is a potent tool in interviews. If you start from the back of your chair you can lean forward either to listen more intently or to show conviction.

- Leakage gestures can be fatal. You may have prepared your verbal answers to those tricky questions like 'Why did you leave your last job?' and 'Talk me through this year-long gap in your CV', but it will be the body language that gives the game away every time.

  Defensive barriering, like folding your arms or leaning away; fiddling with jewellery or body parts, rocking or leg-swinging, will imply there's more to the situation than you are letting on. Too much leg-swinging or neck-rubbing and they'll think the year off was spent in prison, rather than back-packing.

- Remember there is scope for individuality, even within the rather formal framework, so don't police your gestures too severely. You are allowed to move and to express yourself readily. Only sit still if you are completely frozen with fear and suspect that if you moved at all you would flap about like an idiot.

- Learn to live through the pauses. Interviews are full of them and they can be a very nightmarish proposition if, like me, you were brought up believing a pause to be some sort of social disaster. You will need to pause to consider each question before you answer. The interviewer will pause to assimilate – and even write down – your answer. When you are in this latter type of pause, go back to your prime position.

- Never interrupt, not even with your gestures. No hand-raising or manic nodding.

- And never do that thing that candidates specialise in, which is the spreading smile of delight halfway through a question when they realise they know the answer. This technique stinks. It suggests the interviewer is using a cliché and that you are smugly sitting there with a prepared answer. Whenever I spotted that smile I used to bend the question into a massive U-turn.

- Flatter the questioner by listening intently throughout the question. Even frown slightly. This makes it look as though it was a clever question, even if it was old enough to need a Zimmer and stairlift just to get into the room.

▶ Difficult Questions

Tricky questions don't become less tricky if you ignore them and hope they will go away, or never arise in the first place. So arm yourself with one of the many publications providing lists of tough interview questions and prepare your answers to all the relevant ones. Never allow yourself to go into an interview hoping that something won't be asked. This is like Clinton hoping they wouldn't ask him whether he had sex with Monica Lewinsky. If they might ask something, they probably will, and you should rehearse, rehearse, rehearse.

If you are applying for internal promotion you will be even more aware of the catch-out questions. Both you and the interviewer will know where the bodies are buried and when they will start to smell. Ignoring the stink is fruitless. You could do worse than bring any big negative issues up yourself, rather than pretending they don't exist.

Whatever your gambit, rehearse your verbal and visual responses, just as Clinton did. If possible, get family members to role-play, throwing worst-case scenario questions your way so that you can prepare your responses.

Avoid anything that looks or sounds like ducking and diving. Flannel doesn't work these days and neither does dodging the issue. Look and sound as though you have nothing to hide. Lack of experience, a less than healthy track record, past failures – any or all of these should be dealt with if not comfortably, then at least openly and honestly.

Be comfortable with selling yourself. Sit in front of a mirror and practise telling yourself what your strengths are and what your achievements have been to date. Use eye contact and open gestures, but avoid anything that looks smug or arrogant. Work on your techniques until you manage to look at ease with your own body when saying you are good at something.

This book is not specifically aimed at verbal communication, but watch your words nevertheless – particularly words like: 'just', 'sort of', 'we' and 'only'. 'I managed a team of 10 through the successful community project' sounds better than 'We just worked on the community project last year, which sort of finished OK.'

Work on body language that will endorse your words. You may swear you have commitment, but you won't show it if you are sitting back in your chair with your arms folded at the time.

▶ Ending the Interview

The interview will usually end with the interviewer asking if you have any questions. Avoid the shrug at this point. Breathe in, think, either ask something interesting or tell them they seem to have covered everything. Pause. Smile.

As the interviewer gets up, you should rise gracefully to your feet. Never rush or look relieved that the interview is over. Pick up your bag, turn towards the interviewer and follow as they take you towards the door. Be prepared to shake hands again as you leave, but don't instigate it.

Some interviewers don't show you out. They do a kind of half gesture that signals the interview is at an end and that you should leave. This usually consists of the half-rise from the chair. They hold the chair arms and raise their bottoms while keeping their heads low. It looks like an impromptu imitation of a suddenly constipated chicken. If you see this, rise carefully, again without rushing, and stand facing your interviewer and smiling politely for a couple of seconds. Thank them, look for a handshake (there may not be one), turn and leave.

▶ Appraisal Interviews

An appraisal can be difficult for both parties. Giving feedback that is positive can be a joy, but giving and receiving negative feedback can be embarrassing and possibly devastating.

As the manager, your ability to get your message across in the most effective way will be marred by one main factor: your own embarrassment. Nobody likes breaking bad news. And nobody likes taking it, either. As the person called into the meeting, you may go along expecting bad news and this may make you tense and wary. We all like to think we can take criticism on the chin but most of us find even the smallest negative comment severely wounding.

All this tension on both sides can make effective communication difficult.

Managers should consider using Layout 2 *(see page 201)* to add more of a counselling flavour to the meeting.

The manager's body language should never reflect any inner embarrassment or awkwardness at having to criticise or break bad news. The impression you need to give is that you are on the level. The easiest way to disprove this is to start by supplying fawning praise for anything the employee happens to have done right. Praise before the punch can be useful if it is done subtly, but going overboard will only scar future relationships. Next time you praise that person's work they will think they're in for some heavy criticism.

To begin with, using assertive eye contact and with open gestures or your hands lightly clasped together on the desk or on your lap, go through some of the more positive aspects of your meeting.

Avoid an overly-sympathetic pose, as this will make you look patronising. Think of Margaret Thatcher during any TV interview. Head tilted, weak, kindly smile, eye shape softened to signal sympathy, hands steepled in a pious-looking manner, etc . . .

Avoid looking evasive, too. Never shuffle papers or stare at your hands.

As you go through your litany of praise, keep in mind the other person will be waiting for the bad stuff. They will hear it coming a mile off. This is part of the game, unfortunately. If you do too good a job of the praise, they will be expecting promotion or a pay rise and the bad news will hurt even more.

When you start to present the negative comments, be positive with your body language. Lean forward slightly, keeping the eye contact and the open gestures. 'Positive' doesn't mean 'fawning', though. If you sound too positive, they may not see the seriousness of your criticism.

Keep your objective in mind. What is your purpose in raising this subject? What behaviour do you want this person to improve? Criticism should always be specific, rather than general. Keep to the point and don't add hints or non-specifics.

It is important your body language shows you are in control of the meeting, but not aggressive or overbearing. Show that you are prepared to listen as well as speak, but don't allow the other person to dominate with excuses and counter-accusations.

Keep calm and show that quality. Less movement is better than more. If the other person becomes upset you can be sympathetic, but never become flustered or back down as if your viewpoint is over-flexible. Use slow nods to signal you are listening and raise both hands (a low raise, only just above the desk) with fingers flat to close the other person down if they are trying to argue.

Repeating your point over and over is a technique used in assertiveness. You can do the same with your body language. Use the same set of in-control, calming gestures if the other person begins to get upset or heated.

If tears start, stay unrattled. Tears can be caused by anger as well as misery. Pause to allow the other person time to compose themselves and offer a hankie, but avoid going for the hug or even the arm-pat. Many bosses keep a box of tissues nearby in their desk drawer to offer in the case of tears. I find something a little too slick about this. Pulling the Kleenex out too easily implies you reduce staff to blubbing on a regular basis and were almost expecting that response. Pretend to have to reach or hunt for them a bit. It looks better.

There is no perfect way to present truly dreadful news, like involuntary redundancy. Remember the employee may be devastated, but that they may not reflect that in their body language. The struggle to come to grips with the news or mask a response can often produce a smile, laugh, aggression, abuse or other emotions that can appear quite bizarre to the inexperienced. Never try to mirror the emotions being displayed. Portray concern and regret and stick to that. The relief on finding the 'victim' is laughing at the news can often lead to the manager joining in, which is, needless to say, never appropriate. The victim is probably showing a shock response. They won't remember their own reaction later, only yours.

Mirroring can, however, be a useful ploy for a manager dealing with a nervous or unsure member of staff. If your employee is sitting in a very barriered way, with arms crossed and eyes turned away, begin by keeping your own signals more closed. To get them to relax more, you can lead by gradually opening out your own gestures and relaxing in your own seat. With luck – and without realising what they are doing – they will usually begin to relax as well.

This skill of leading applies for most kinds of interview. If it is the objective of the interviewer to get the most out of the interviewee, they can do so by this 'copy-then-change' style.

Key Points in a Nutshell

▶ Rehearse your interview bodytalk until you are able to look natural, confident and relaxed. The more you practise, the more these techniques will be programmed into your 'muscle memory', so that you will be able to do them even if you feel nervous on the day.

▶ Visualise yourself doing well, with positive facial expressions and gestures.

▶ Leave nothing to chance – select bag and outfit and do a dress rehearsal to see how they move as well.

▶ Interviewers need to put in just as much work. Plan the layout of the room to the best advantage of both sides and work out the choreography, especially if you are conducting a panel interview.

Chapter 15

*M*eetings and Team Working

ALTHOUGH EVERYONE OPERATES fundamentally as a loner at work, led by personal desires and motivations we might not even be aware of, there is also a need in most jobs for the eponymous 'team working'.

The idea, as you probably already know, is that teams achieve more than individuals. Throw people into a random group and somewhere along the line their mutual strengths will outweigh their individual weaknesses.

This, of course, depends on the dynamics of the team. If it works, great. If not, disaster. Any team, no matter how hand-picked and honed, can be brought down if there is an outbreak of whingeing, bitching, favoritism, office politics, laziness, nega-tivity, stupidity, internal competition, power-posturing, back-stabbing . . . in fact, all and any of the usual suspects.

The speed of modern business means that teams are more transitory than they once were. Instant bonding calls for special skills, yet all too often there is little conscious realisation that there is a team at all. I have seen groups of bewildered staff thrown together on team-building courses, staring blinking and bemused at one another.

A team is a pack. You only have to watch the wildlife pro-grammes on TV to see the advantages and disadvantages of pack mentality. Real packs mean trouble for the competition because they fight more effectively than an individual. But watch them turn on each other once the enemy has scarpered.

Pack behaviour at work is not dependent on physical strength, which makes the pecking order even more uneasy. Age is rarely a consideration. Youth can lead over age and experience. Females can be put in charge of males who may be physically dominant. Aggressive pack members may be forced to submit to passive and weak bosses. Put the same group on a survival week in the heart of the rain-soaked moors and you will usually see a complete reversal of roles.

What is fascinating, though, is the difference between the bestowed status of the work pack member and the 'actual' pecking orders of the team. Status at work is often awarded against the natural tendencies of the group, or there may be no official team-leader at all and so the pecking order becomes random and stormy. Fights will break out, but they will rarely if ever become fisticuffs, because: a) we are civilised human beings, and b) it would mean dismissal. So most of them are played out on the field of non-verbal communication.

Watch any group for a period of time and you will see signs of transitory or ongoing power-struggles. Many of these wars are pointless because the winner has already been appointed and that is non-negotiable. And yet we still battle away, engulfed in skirmishes that we may not even be aware of ourselves.

Effective teams need an equilibrium, no matter how uneasy. The perfect team will have balance, with each member aware of their role and happy to add that value to the task. The natural leader for any given job will be in charge and their leadership will be cherished by mutual consent. Being a perfect team member means commitment to the task overrides personal ambition and glory. Unfortunately this is rarely achieved in the workplace.

So, how to win at team games?

First, be aware of the underlying power struggles. Each time the team meets the pecking order will be reinforced or challenged. Notice where people sit and how they position themselves.

Study your own goals within the team. Do you truly want to be a team-player or will you have your own agenda? Do you want to see the team succeed or would you prefer it to fail, if it suits your own profile? Be honest here. Don't trot out the usual corporate brain-washing. Even if you put your own needs first, you can still decide to commit to the team ethics and dynamics.

To succeed in a team and as a team you need to reaffirm your current role within it to yourself. A winger in football will not play well within the team if he spends his time wishing he were in goal.

Your visual approach as a team-member needs to be one of maintained equilibrium. People show themselves up in team meetings by either alienating themselves from the group ('I'm not playing'), or unnecessarily and strenuously dominating.

You will alienate yourself if you:

▶ sit away from the others

▶ turn your body away

▶ cross your legs and your arms to form a visual barrier

▶ look away

▶ only speak when asked a question

▶ whisper or send body language signals exclusively to one other member of the team

▶ pass notes to that other person (yes, it does sound childish, but it happens all the time in team meetings)

▶ pull your chair out in front of the group – this assumption of leadership may be too defined for some group goals and dis-cussions or briefings in the round will often be more effective

▶ sit at the back.

You will perform as part of the team if you:

▶ Share your responses evenly. Sit or stand in a central position. Look at the entire group during any discussions. Spread your eye contact evenly.

▶ Show evenly-spread listening skills and alert-looking body language. Watch the others while you are not communicating verbally and even when you do talk, scan the entire team for responses to your comments.

▶ Don't battle the team leader. When the team is focused on a task the warfare should wait. There is no need to grovel, but you should show a level of respect. Show you are listening by using visual listening signals. Avoid body language stand-offs like folded arms, hands on hips or taking the more dominant sitting/standing position at the top of the table or middle of the group.

▶ Don't battle within the group. Monitor skills and resources at all times. Allow team members with stronger skills to do the appropriate jobs. Mask your disappointment if the jobs were ones you wanted.

A pack will tend to move together. Assuming your team isn't running across open fields and turning on sixpence, your choreographed 'pack' movements will be subtle. You may all lean forward at roughly the same time or laugh or relax your posture together. This group 'mirroring' is a vital ingredient of the well-oiled team.

▶ Business Meetings

I love business meetings because I don't have to attend them, except as a behavioural observer. I view people who do attend on a regular basis with the same amount of pity as I would animals locked in the zoo. The words 'boring' and 'warfare' are rarely if ever used together but 'boring warfare' is the only way I can describe most business meetings.

On the one hand you are called to account for yourself and create a good impression. Your opinions need to be inspired and intelligent and so does the way in which you put them across. On the other hand you are engaged in a power battle with nearly everyone else in the room. But above all else you are having to struggle to stay awake.

Regular meetings inspire serial behaviour patterns. People sit in the same seats, in the same way, taking the same stances and acquiring the same stereotyped character. This is something you should avoid like the plague.

Meeting Success

Generally, your body language at business meetings needs to meet some very simple criteria to create a good image:

▶ Arrive on time.

▶ Enter the room looking energetic and keen (the others will love this because it is contagious and will re-energise the entire group).

▶ If you do arrive late, make a good entrance. Never rush in looking flustered or apologetic. Say sorry once, give a brief reason if necessary, but never go into gory details. You've held them up enough as it is.

▶ Greet everyone warmly but quickly.

▶ Choose your seat carefully. Each position around the table has its own power and energy status *(see page 76 and below)*.

▶ Settle yourself quickly.

▶ Choose the way you sit carefully. Meetings become a dance of group dynamics, usually led by the highest-status person in the room.

▶ Look interested in the agenda.

▶ Once the meeting has started, give it your complete attention – don't start pouring coffee, reaching for biscuits or thumbing through papers. Someone else will be speaking and the effect is always distracting. It will put them off their stride.

▶ Speak up within the first few minutes. Get used to the sound of your own voice in the room. The longer you leave it, the less likely you will be to say anything.

▶ Use body language to announce that you want to speak. Lean forward, looking other colleagues in the eye, and place your hands or arms on the table, or raise one hand in a 'closing' gesture. If your group tends to be boisterous, raise both hands or stick your pen up in the air.

▶ If you find it difficult to break in, remember attention from others is usually earned, rather than given as a right, so work on your reputation. Make each point you do make concise, to the point, interesting and positive. Serial whingers or diffident speakers will usually be excluded on a regular basis unless they happen to have the initials MD after their name.

▶ Put energy into every point you make. Meetings are boring enough without a flat monologue.

▶ Look at everyone in turn as you speak; don't leave anyone out.

▶ Never start with a verbal disclaimer like 'I know I'm always keeping on about this, but . . .'

▶ Never use body language disclaimers like dismissive hand waves, apologetic fiddling or hand-rubbing, or head-shaking.

▶ When you are stumped for a comment, join in visually. Employ all the visual listening skills described earlier, only soup them up a notch.

▶ When someone else is talking – look at them and respond visually to what they are saying.

▶ Never whisper to any other colleagues while someone else is speaking.

▶ Avoid taking copious notes or it will look as though you are taking minutes.

▶ Never put more items on the boardroom table than the leader you are trying to impress.

▶ Never pour the coffee if you can help it or go round with the biscuits. It gives you a low-status nurturing visual role.

▶ Never show up looking ill or tired. It destroys the entire energy of the group.

▶ Always turn your mobile off.

▶ End the meeting with the same energy. Pack up quickly and never nick sweets, biscuits or fruit to take back to the office. If you need to pick off a colleague for individual discussion, try not to ambush them. Ask if they have a few minutes and talk together outside the meeting room.

▶ Thank anyone who has been taking minutes or serving refreshments.

Table-turning

Your seat at the table needs to give you the best chance to follow your agenda. Pick up a pen right now and write down your honest, inner motives at in-house business meetings. Select from ideas like:

▶ impress the boss

▶ suck up to the boss

▶ act like the boss

▶ I am the boss and I want everyone to respect that

▶ sell my best ideas

▶ keep quiet and try to be ignored

▶ challenge others

▶ create havoc.

I'll stop there, but you needn't. All I ask is that you're honest with yourself.

The next step is to discover how group dynamics work and what each position might mean:

▶ The power seats

As mentioned earlier, the highest in status will usually sit in one of two positions: at the end of the table or in the middle of the long side, facing the door. These are the power seats.

▶ Directly opposite the long end

Sitting in this position, at the opposite end of a long board table, can imply direct conflict. It also means you are the one who is most excluded from the inner sanctum. If your aim is to impress, then you have picked the wrong seat. You will be the hardest to hear, while supplying an almost baleful presence.

▶ Directly opposite widthways

This is the most visible spot, but there may be a conscious effort to ignore the person sitting in it. You block all the boss's energy by sitting directly opposite and create an almost one-to-one visual dialogue that the boss may be at pains to avoid, as it excludes the others. This is the 'stalker' seat, for borderline obsessive fans or toady-merchants.

▶ Beside the boss

This is where quiet fawning can be done and you can sit and pull 'I'm the favourite' faces at the rest of the group. If you sit here you will look silently supportive. It is usually reserved for finance directors and accountants with grave faces and little to say to themselves.

The point to remember is that you are in the boss's blind spot, so they may not even be aware of your presence, and when you do make a point they may be at great pains to disassociate themselves from it, as they may feel you look too much like their spokesperson.

▶ Along the middle diagonals

These spots are quite handy for ducking in and out at will. If the boss is the tip of the triangle and you sit at one of the two bottom points you should command maximum attention without looking like a toady or a challenge to their power.

▶ Along the further diagonals.

This is getting a bit more frosty. You will have to shout more loudly to be heard and you can be too easily sidelined.

▶ Boss in middle, you at either far end

You are in Antarctica. Your charisma will need to be industrial-force to blast in from that distance.

There is no need to fret if you get stuck with a bad position, however. Any seat can be turned to your advantage if you keep your objectives in mind and keep the balance with your body language.

Boardroom Moves

If you feel your position provides unwanted conflict with a colleague, make your posture less assertive. Look at the person you feel there is a problem with. What is their position like?

Aggression or confrontation around a boardroom table can be shown by:

▶ leaning forward, elbows on table and chin slightly raised

▶ leaning forward over folded arms

▶ peering over glasses

▶ steepling fingers

▶ sitting back, arms folded

▶ sitting back, hands behind head.

The first two can register disagreement that is challenging and relatively open. If you feel you are up to the challenge you could mirror, but without raising your chin.

The second two poses imply high-status disapproval or a judgemental attitude. Never mirror these. Maintain your pose and do not give way. You probably just need to be more persuasive in your arguments.

The last two imply your idea is being quashed or ridiculed. Watch the eye contact with the last pose. If they are still glancing at your proposal it could just mean it is a difficult decision. If they look around the table or try to catch the eye of the boss with this pose they are probably trying to signal to everyone else that they think your idea is rubbish.

Keep calm. At this point it is probably best to ask the person what their reservations are. This implies you can take any queries and are confident of supplying a good answer. It also means they will probably drop their arms back on to the table, which will restore some of the positive dynamics. If this doesn't work, have some spare documents to hand to them, to ensure the arms come down as they take them from you. This engineered change of pose will have given you back the control. While they are reading, go on with the point you were making.

▶ Tele-conferencing

Body language plays little part here. Business people sit in far-flung corners of the Empire and participate in a virtual meeting. This is great if the voices range from between Sean Connery bass to a piping contralto, because then you will have instant recognition of who it is talking. Unfortunately this is rarely the case. Then you have the problem with 'no-talks' and 'talk-overs'. Huge pauses emerge when everyone waits for someone else to speak, little realising all the others have hopped off to the loo or to collect a quick coffee. Then there is a rush to speak, when two or more people overlap. This is because they cannot read the 'break-in' body language signals.

Interestingly, many home phones have this facility and even a lot of mobiles are fitted with it. So, rehearse your techniques with your family and friends, ready for the business calls.

▶ Video Conferencing

This can be difficult. I have been on news programmes where I have sat alone in a studio, talking straight into a camera, while listening to the voice of the presenter hundreds of miles away. It is not an easy technique to master.

Have you had corporate photos taken? The result is often the same. You stare at a piece of equipment, forgetting that you should be looking at it as though it were human. Even if you are face-to-face with the caller on your screen, you will probably forget and think the image is one-way. Remember those photographs. How closely did your expression resemble a rabbit caught in the headlights of a car, two seconds before it became roadkill?

Again, if this practice becomes commonplace you are going to have to rehearse in a 'safe' environment first, until your expression looks human and you remember to comb your hair before picking the phone up.

Key Points in a Nutshell

▶ Team techniques entail generosity. Avoid displays of overt individual 'bettering'. Play with the pack.

▶ Study group dynamics – playing a room with your bodytalk is never the same as working one-to-one.

▶ Meeting techniques include ways of introducing your communication and long-term signalling, plus building a historical reputation for good-value communication, both visual and verbal.

Chapter 16

*B*usiness Presentations

EVERYONE LOATHES PRESENTING, apart from the show-offs. Funnily enough, the audience hates presentations almost as much as the speaker. This is because most of them are deeply, gut-numbingly boring. Rule number 1: Keep it as interesting as possible.

Presentations come in roughly four sizes:

1. One-to-one briefings

2. Talking to small groups informally

3. More formal talks to groups

4. The big on-stage conference variety

Show-offs like me enjoy conferences best, but they scare a lot of people witless. Most of this thinking comes from whether you are an optimist or a pessimist. If you are the first you believe people will like you and enjoy your talk. Having a vast group of people like you is therefore much more fun. Pessimists, meantime, assume the audience hates them. A large group is just too much hatred to handle.

This book focuses on the body language involved in presentations, but here are just a few quick general tips as well:

- ▸ Learn how to structure your talk.

- ▸ Write your own talk and use your own visuals.

- ▸ Do exercises and training to boost your confidence and self-esteem.

- ▸ Find out as much as you can about your audience and about the content of any other talks at the same conference.

▶ Preparation

Any communication where you are speaking centre-stage should be planned beforehand. Small, informal talks to small groups or one-to-one need about as much in the way of preparation as the big events. One person in your audience is every bit as important as 50.

Numbers do change dynamics, though. The smaller the audience, the easier it will be to read their bodytalk signals. If there are fewer than 15 people in your audience, you should get them to participate. If the group is larger, it will become more of a pack. This can be positive, so don't let the word 'pack' bring to mind hunting, ripping to shreds and eating.

One of the first tricks of presenting is to become less 'me' obsessed. Yes, they *are* all looking at you and in a way judging you and your message, but the less you think about that, the better. When you present you need to be polite and mindful of others. Your head should be full of 'How do they feel?', rather than 'How do I look?' So work on your bodytalk techniques. Practise talking in front of a mirror while standing empty-handed. Gesticulate as you make points. Smile. The sooner you learn to consign your new posture and gestures to the subconscious auto-pilot of muscle memory, the better.

▶ Layout

No matter how large or small your audience, it is important you get a chance to take control of the room. The success of your presentation depends on it. Never assume the layout will be OK. Usually it isn't.

One-to-one presenting may need a more casual 'interview-style' layout or you might need to half-stand in front of the other person's chair. This is assuming you are the one running the session. You may have been called into a firm to pitch to the MD, in which case the layout may be that of a normal, formal presentation.

Standing while the other person sits can create threatening body language, which is why you will need to gauge the most comfortable space between the two of you. If you stand too close to your listener's chair you will appear to loom over them.

The half-prop can be useful in situations where the talk is semi-casual but needs a presentation-style approach. A table is a handy place to perch, but only if you have checked beforehand that it will take your weight and support you without wobbling.

If your presentation is to be held boardroom-style, then good luck, because you're going to need it. Most tables fill the room they are in and you often find yourself placed up the far end with the wall behind you. This is probably the least comfortable position invented, for both you and the audience. They will often sit with their chairs facing the table and their heads swivelled round in your direction. You feel like a fly pinned against the wallpaper. The board table dominates and becomes the star. I always mean to carry a small axe in my briefcase to deal with board tables that I am asked to present around. If it is possible to have the table dismantled beforehand and stored in a nearby room, then do it.

If you are attending a meeting around a table and are asked to present your points, stand to talk when possible. When you stand you increase your impact 100 per cent.

One finance manager I trained had to attend weekly meetings where the other directors routinely gave him a savaging when he presented the figures. He had started to dread the meetings and his body language was extremely defensive. I got him to prepare his facts more fully beforehand and to take along a prepared flip chart with graphs and figures printed professionally on it. The flip chart provided the excuse he felt he needed to get up from the table and stand during his talk. His body language became more authoritative and, because he was better prepared, he could bring up and deal with objections before his audience did. Magically, they stopped giving him a hard time.

When deciding whether to present sitting or standing, think of your audience and the impact of your message, not your own comfort. If your prime concern were your own comfort, you would probably choose to present from underneath the table if that were possible. It isn't. Get up there and get your message across.

If the boardroom is spacious, present from the far end of the table but turn all the chairs to face you and fan them out, so that every member of the audience can see you comfortably.

If you are presenting from the long side, stand in the middle and try to move all the seats so that they are facing you. The 'dead' seats will be the ones on either side of you.

The best arrangement for larger groups is the horseshoe shape. If the room is large and the group not too big, try to arrange the U-shape in a single line.

Rows of seats should only be used if necessary because the people in the back rows will rarely participate well without strenuous encouragement. Most speakers end up with an empty front row as well. To avoid this, either arrange for people to be led into the front seats first or for some members of your own group to sit there if possible.

Always be aware of the comfort space between yourself and the front row. If you are a speaker who moves around a lot, you should make the space you will be working in as wide as possible. Always avoid feeling trapped against the wall or your equipment.

If the room needs to be set up in multiple rows you should still try to keep these in the shape of a U. Even if you move a lot, you only take up a small amount of room at the front and straight rows will always mean 'dead' seats at the outer edges.

I find lecture theatres the most daunting, possibly because I don't work in many of them. I prefer to be higher than my audience and feel in a bit of a bear-pit looking up at all those tiers.

Working on a stage can be exciting, but you will need to 'tread the boards' to get the feel of the space and height before the conference starts. Never balk at a full rehearsal, with the same lighting and microphone set-up that has been arranged for your talk. Nothing looks worse than a speaker blinking and wincing into the spotlight as they start their talk and then looking startled by their own amplified voice.

Check out the position of all the equipment you will be using, including light switches and dimmers, power sockets and blinds. Make sure there are no bare leads or cables for you to trip over. Unless you are working with back projection, make sure none of your visual aids block the audience's view.

Find out how you will make your entrance and whether you will be announced. Check out how you will get miked up, if necessary. If you are given a choice, go for a lapel mike every time. They move with you and the hand-held variety tie up your gestures, while making you look as though you are about to do a chorus of 'My Way' for karaoke night. Sound engineers can be stingy with the amount of mikes they order. I have often arrived to be told that I will have to use the last speaker's mike, once they have taken it off. What they often fail to add is that they intend to do the swap in front of the audience. Do not – repeat, do not – go there. The mike wire will be hauled up out of the last speaker's pants and then you will be forced to shove it down the front of your own jacket, then stand there while they rummage up the back of your clothes to fix the transmitter to the waistband of your knickers. This is not the coolest way to begin an important speech. Ask for your own mike, but make sure it isn't turned on too soon. One speaker I worked with was waiting while her audience arrived to fill the auditorium and quietly asked the chairperson why the fattest ones always sat in the front row. Unfortunately the mike was on and the whole room heard her.

▶ Visual Aids

Only use these to enhance your talk. Plan and rehearse your presentation without them and then only introduce them as necessary. Too many talks are structured around the visual aids. They then become a crutch for the speaker and upstage the whole talk. This may sound tempting to the terminally nervous, but it is not the best option, believe me. Remember you are selling a message and what the audience need to buy from is you. Visuals can enhance or emphasise, but they can never persuade or portray energy and commitment.

Your visual aids should always be controlled by, rather than controlling, you. Use them smoothly and easily. Mistakes and breakdowns can be almost inevitable, but should never faze you. That's why you should always be able to talk without them.

Some more tips:

▸ Keep your visuals simple. Never use any you will have to apologise for, as in 'This one is a little busy' or 'I'm sorry if you can't quite read all that's on that one' etc.

▸ If you are using Power Point or overheads, create even lighting so that your visuals can be seen, but you aren't left talking from the gloom.

▸ Never turn to read off your screen or flip chart, or to stare at it for inspiration. Switch it off or show a blank screen while you are not using it.

▸ Learn to write on your flip chart without turning your back.

▶ Props

Where possible, present centre-stage, with nothing between you and your audience. Never read from a script and never hold notes or cue cards. If you are doing a big production talk, then learn to use an autocue. If not, keep your notes on a table nearby and only refer back to them when you have to.

Lecterns are always a bit of a nightmare. Only ever contemplate using one if the audience is very large or you are briefing newsmen from the White House. Lecterns create a barrier, but remember your legs and feet may still be visible. One HR manager I work with was invited to a seminar by a leading trainer. She said he gave a good talk, but only from the chest up. Standing behind his lectern he obviously didn't realise his legs were visible in the mirror behind. While he spoke he was slipping in and out of his shoes and rubbing one leg against the other. It became the main focus of a good part of the audience.

▶ Top Tips

- ▶ Warm up before you go on. Exercise the vocal chords and do a breathing and flexing work-out.

- ▶ Wear clothes that you can move in. Suit and shoes must feel comfortable but they should also be smart and well-groomed. Don't touch your clothing while you are presenting and never 'dress yourself', i.e. do up buttons, hike up trousers or straighten ties, while you are in front of your audience.

- ▶ Empty your pockets. Never have anything in there you can play with.

- ▶ Empty the surrounding area of 'toys'. Pointers, paperclips, ornaments – it's amazing what you will pick up and play with when you feel anxious.

- ▶ Take mental control of your space before you speak by moving something, even if you just straighten a chair or adjust the position of the flip chart.

- ▶ Never think you have to leave things where the last speaker put them. Move stuff if you want.

- ▶ Get into your prime position to start your talk. This is one you have worked on in front of the mirror at home. Your weight should be evenly balanced on both feet, your posture pulled up and hands held lightly in front.

- ▶ Stand in the middle of the speaking spot, facing your audience squarely, when you start.

- ▶ Avoid 'twee' positions, i.e. legs crossed and hands held high in the hamster pose.

- ▶ Look pleased to see your audience. Smile and use eye contact as you introduce yourself.

▶ Everyone in the UK – with the exception of the Queen – is expected to be funny when talking in public. Even a mass murderer would win over the British if he could inject a little self-effacing humour into his conversation. So, if you can make your audience, laugh, cry and go away with a handful of key points, you can be out there earning thousands of pounds per lecture on the corporate circuit. If you are not naturally funny, though, don't try to be. Give your talk with a straight-faced delivery and quit while you are ahead.

▶ Exaggerate your tone and exaggerate your body language signals, but avoid changing your natural style more than is necessary.

▶ Break any rule you have ever read about presenting. If it works, go for it. A hand in the pocket, pacing about the stage, arm-waving gesticulations, folding your arms – all of these can look good if done in a stylish manner.

▶ Look at your audience, but don't stare at anyone too directly or for too long. Exclude nobody, but don't work on a mechanical 'sweep' – distribute fairly but naturally.

▶ Always be on the alert for a question from the audience. Never look defensive by backing away or creating body-barriers as you answer. Walk out towards the questioner, repeat the question if it is a large room, and never bluff it out if you don't know the answer.

▶ Avoid verbal and gestural inflation. There is no need for you to pretend to be passionate about everything and if you inflate constantly you will find you have nowhere to go when the really important or exciting bits come up.

▶ Like your visual aids, your gestures should be used to enhance your message and emphasise your words. Avoid the annoyingly repetitive, the hugely distracting or the unfinished gesture, like an incomplete steeple or an unused pen with the top pulled off.

▶ Never be unnecessarily formal. There is no need to expect that the larger the group, the more formal your style needs to be. Only vary your delivery according to the subject-matter.

▶ Never allow yourself the luxury of 'warming up as you go along'. Did you ever leave a play praising the actors for 'warming up in the second half'? People in business are busy. Their time is precious. You owe it to them to hit the ground running.

Key Points in a Nutshell

▶ Rehearse your body language as well as your verbal message.

▶ Never rely on visual aids. Learn to present without them first.

▶ Monitor your audience's body language as well as your own.

---

Chapter 17

*F*ace-to-face with Customers

H OW YOU TREAT your customers will depend very much on the type of product or service your business delivers, but dealing with any sort of external customer means you need well-honed communication skills. You need to be adept at both reading their outgoing signals and responding with your own.

▶ Receptionists and Front-line Staff

A receptionist's prime objective is to greet customers and visitors, creating a good impression of the company as they do so. This means a genuine-looking smile, a slight forward lean on greeting to signal a desire to help and an immediate nod of acknowledgement, even when you are busy. Receptionists need to be pro-active, observing customers waiting and dealing with any problems before they arise. Some, particularly medical receptionists, also have to deal well with stress and complaint. Most of the skills needed hark back to the body language principle 'observe and respond'.

If there are two receptionists sitting at a desk and one is busy, the customer will assume the other is free to deal with them. If not, the result is anger. Visually it is always better to have an unmanned public seat than one that is used by someone who isn't available.

This is why you should never sit in reception to eat lunch and why banks should try to move staff round the back to work, rather than sitting them at the counter but making them unavailable to clients.

As with any other job, the desk layout is important in reception. One of the most high-impact factors is the chair–desk height ratio. Hotel receptions rarely provide seats, which means the customer is greeted eyeball-to-eyeball and there is a sense of energy and commitment in the non-static gestures.

Most other receptions provide chairs. The ideal seat will keep the receptionist's face even with the customer's, so that the greeting is effective as some feeling of energy and possible activity is maintained. The lower the chair sinks and the higher the desk rises, the greater the barrier between customer and receptionist, both physically and emotionally. Low seat and high desk says, 'Push off, I'm nesting.'

With any sort of front-line work, it's important to attune your mood and approach to your product. That sounds easy enough, doesn't it? You wouldn't sit giggling on the desk in Intensive Care while relatives were arriving to enquire whether a loved one had made it through the night, would you? If you were a policeman with a highly distressed woman waiting to speak to you you'd never stop for a quick joke with a policewoman before attending to her, would you? Or be irritated by a client with a heavy foreign accent in immigration control? Yet all of these things have happened.

The key is to think out the whole process for the customers you are dealing with. Imagine how they feel when they meet you. Go outside and walk into the building as though you were the customer. How does it look? What do you want? Hotel guests, for example, are usually tired from travelling and slightly confused. They want a friendly greeting and to feel that they are being taken care of. Acknowledge, smile and listen – these are the main visual skills you need to work on.

▶ The Medical and Beauty Professions

The big difference in body language when you work in the medical or beauty professions is the change in rules of touch and closeness. Doctors, nurses and beauticians are professional touchers. The customer is submissive, dependent and often stripped of their dignity as well. You need instant trust and rapport. Fortunately, you will probably have the customer helping you because it is in their interests as well.

Listening, caring and authority are perhaps the most frequently used blend of visual signals in the health sector. A doctor will need to gain speedy and accurate information from the patient and to be adept at reading between the lines when a patient says they only consume two units of alcohol and smoke 10 cigarettes a week. Patient responses are also probably the most misleading. People who are ill are perfectly able to look brave when they are in agony, shrug things off when they are anxious and nod understanding when they are barely able to listen.

Listening to the Customer: The 'Listen and Log' Syndrome

Like any complaining client, a patient's prime need is to be listened to. Unfortunately, the doctor's attention is often turned away from the patient to the computer screen. Talking to someone who is tapping a keyboard while staring at the screen is hard. Even when the conscious mind knows what is happening here, the ability to communicate is inhibited. The response you have been taught since childhood will start to kick in – that when you don't have someone's full attention you should stop speaking. They aren't listening.

There are ways around this, though. I have watched radio hosts at work and the best ones handle this problem well by exaggerating their listening signals to flatter and encourage. If their eyes have to leave your face to fiddle with a switch, they nod intensely. They respond to every funny comment as though it were hilarious. When they are free to watch you, the hand goes on the chin and the concerned, interested facial expression, complete with nodding, is foolproof. Other 'quick listeners' in business can do the same.

Some listening skills tips:

▶ Display intense listening for some part of the conversation and definitely at the start. Use eye contact, nodding and mirroring to show the client that you are paying full attention.

▶ If you need to write or use the PC, explain what you are doing, even if you think it must be obvious.

▶ If possible, have the screen in the 'share' position and point something out on the patient's notes so that they can see for themselves.

▶ Avoid the 'type and then stare during a question routine'. I have even seen a GP look at the patient over the top of her glasses at this point. It gives the patient the impression of being quizzed in quite an aggressive manner.

▶ Time is obviously hugely tight, but going straight from a PC to a medical examination is like sex without the foreplay. Spend a few seconds doing face-to-face chat before the touching starts.

▶ Offering Help

Helping others is more difficult than might seem at first sight. Never assume that help is wanted, even when it is needed. Many people hate being dependent on others. The greatest technique to learn is how to offer help without taking the higher-status patronising stance.

Children, old people, needy people and those who are ill all deserve to be treated with respect. As with other people, the rules of engagement should be dictated by them. They may be quiet, confident, outgoing, diffident or gregarious. There is no 'one size fits all' for your response. Read each person as an individual and respond to their needs in the same way.

With children, go to the same height level where possible. Talk calmly and in a pleasant but grown-up manner. Children think they are tiny adults anyway. There's no need for patronising baby voices and silly words. Mirror a child as you would an adult, toning down eye contact with the shy and copying barrier gestures until the child relaxes and starts to open up.

▶ Creative and Media

These people are free-wheeling, emotional, creative, right-brain thinkers. So if you work with them, be fun, be clever but above all be enthusiastic. A lot of the greatest ideas in the media are also the wildest, so enthusiasm in your delivery style is vital. When media people present an idea they tend to act out the overjoyed response of the customer. To be honest, they can get over-excited.

To fit into media culture you will need to be tuned into the mood swings and peaks. Advertisers will peak around a big client campaign, actors around the opening night of a play. TV and radio people peak with each programme, though they tend to mask their peaks behind a kind of aeroplane pilot-style calm. I have been hauled onto programmes at the last minute and shoved in front of a mike or a camera with literally a couple of seconds to go, but I have never seen one single tantrum from the studio staff. Once you understand the bio-rhythms of the business, then, you can tune your bodytalk to the prevailing culture.

▶ The Public Sector

One of the first things to learn when dealing with the public is that 'people skills' are a prime quality of your job, rather than a by-product. You need to read other people well and then be flexible in your own approach. An open-minded approach is vital, too. Never take it personally when someone complains. The moment this happens the situation becomes a fight and that will show in your eyes, as well as your gestures. If you work in a job that deals regularly with aggression or conflict, but where you have no position of power to defend yourself, you need to become adept at closing conflict down.

Dealing with Difficult Customers

'Empathy' is the key word here. If someone is set on being difficult you are going to have to steer carefully through several vital stages:

1. Be instantly attentive

Whatever you do, even if it is the last thing you do, you are going to have to give them your attention *instantly*. No last few words to finish a conversation with a colleague. No final flick through that magazine you hid beneath the counter. No 'I've got to go' farewell to that personal caller.

Somehow, somewhere, your customer's ego has received a right old pasting. This may have been recent or it may have been in their childhood. Possibly it's a combination of the two. Maybe their mother ignored them when they cried for an ice-cream. And now you're about to ignore them when they've come to bawl for a refund.

Don't.

Any delay is deadly. Each second spent in waiting fills up at least another cubic foot of their madness tanks. There will only be two valid reasons for any delay:

▶ Your own bloody-mindedness. You can see they're borderline ballistic and you want to wind them up. Your own ego took a pasting once and you've been taking it out on po-faced clients ever since.

▶ You are genuinely tied up. Not literally, of course, unless you're in the bondage business, but your new customer is in a queue or waiting while you handle a phone call.

Being otherwise engaged is still no excuse for lack of acknowledgement. So make eye contact and briefly raise your eyebrows, or nod your head, or lift a finger and give a small smile or widen or narrow your eyes slightly. Prolonged eye-widening or narrowing can look aggressive, so make it a fleeting gesture.

2. 'Aerobic listening'

When you do engage the client in conversation you must signal your complete attention. Looking distracted, even for an instant, will lead them to think that you aren't taking the complaint seriously. If you are manning a desk or counter, you may need to get a colleague to take over your position to avoid your having to look away to acknowledge any other arrivals in your queue.

When listening to a complaint, use the following bodytalk:

▸ eye contact

▸ eyebrows lowered in concentration

▸ incline the head or the torso forward slightly

▸ nod slowly

▸ have your hands cupped in front of your waist.

Your expression needs to be one of genuine concern. This is not an easy stunt to pull off and I would suggest a lot of mirror-rehearsal before you unleash your look of concern on the public. It consists of:

▸ a slight frown

▸ one eyebrow lowered and one raised (contortionists only need apply, but it is well worth the practice)

▸ lips slightly parted

▸ head slightly lowered

▸ finger to chin

▸ a hesitant nod of understanding or slight head shake in disbelief (as in 'My God! How awful!', not as in 'You're making all of this up, you liar.')

3. The apology

You will probably apologise, even if the problem was not your fault – after all, the customer is upset. Sincerity is vital at this point, so be careful not to overdo things. Acting as if the customer has just had their entire family wiped out in a chainsaw massacre when they are only reporting a broken heel on a pair of walking shoes will obviously do little for your credibility.

When apologising:

▸ use eye contact but don't bore into the person

▸ lower your chin slightly

- have your hands still clasped at waist height, or held apart, palms facing down, fingers slightly splayed

- the palm-up gesture can signal openness, but be careful as this gesture is becoming a bit of a cliché in business and can appear false or look like denial if used too strenuously.

This last gesture moves you from inactive behaviour, like listening, sympathising and apologising, into active behaviour, like explaining your solution and sorting the problem out.

4. The remedy

Don't be too quick with this one or the customer will think you are rushing them or being glib. Part of the need of a person with a complaint is to be effectively listened to. So the listening and apologising may mean more than the solution. The real problem may be the feeling that the person has been demeaned in some way. This is why the techniques you have employed have been to give a visual effect of self-lowering, without resorting to grovelling.

When describing your solution you can begin to employ more energy with the following:

- variable eye contact (looking away occasionally to think)

- emphatic hand gestures, though still with the hands around waist level, as any higher could seem aggressive or superior

- hands held in more of a palms-up position, varying from palms facing inward like an angler describing their catch as you describe the solution to palms up as you seek approval from the client at the end

- a slight shoulder-shrug, but be careful as too much may signal indifference

- your expression relaxing into a slight smile if the client appears about to accept your suggestion

- head tilting to one side and eyebrows raised again to signal: 'What do you think?'

An element of mirroring should accompany all your techniques. As I have said, this means you will be slightly copying, or being led by, the other person's verbal tone and body language. However, a complaining customer should be mirrored less than the regular type for obvious reasons. Mirroring their anger and distress will simply end in conflict. Your role is to imply confidence but lowered status. The client should always look like the boss.

Tackling Anger

If the complaint turns to anger you have two options: try to pacify or cut and run. I would always suggest the latter if violence seems inevitable, unless you work in a profession like the police, where tackling violence is inevitable.

Ordinary anger that is becoming offensive will usually merit the physical 'close-down'. This is where your gaze is dropped to the floor and a barrier, like folded arms, is put up. The message sent out by these gestures should be that you find the other person's behaviour inappropriate and will only continue to deal with them once it has stopped. This is often a better option than joining in. Allowing the other person to exhaust themselves while you batten down the hatches can diffuse the rage while teaching the culprit that there is nothing to be gained from the bad behaviour.

▶ Selling

All jobs require an ability to sell, yet 'I'm not a salesman!' is a cry heard in all industries and even door-to-door hawkers are now known as 'product consultants'. So what's wrong with selling? If you make a product or supply a service you will need to get someone to buy it, after all.

When you deal with a customer face-to-face, direct-selling a product, you are probably aware of your prime objective. If you only work with internal clients you are still selling yourself and your ideas. You may want to persuade and influence the people you work with. You may also have an unseen influence on external image perception. A company's image is made up from each individual member of staff that it employs. In every communication we are responsible for 'selling' the message.

So don't get too shirty about selling as a concept. It's not a down-market skill.

The Sales Process

There are six main stages to any sales process:

1. Planning
2. Building rapport
3. Listening
4. Telling
5. Selling
6. Reviewing

1. Planning

At this stage you will be finding out everything you can about your customer and their company. Who is the chief decision-maker? Even in shop sales this can be important. If a couple comes in, who is it that will be taking the decision to buy?

You will also be building your own inner self-esteem, learning all you can about your product and any associated products or services your firm delivers and planning the basics of your pitch.

2. Rapport

Building empathy with your customer is vital. You need to show that you are talking the same language. This can be achieved in several ways, but business dress and body language are both vital factors. Tailor your behaviour to suit the people you are talking to. This is the time for small-talk and mirroring.

3. Listening

Customers give us clues about their feelings and thoughts. If you don't pick up these signals, either through self-obsession or arrogance, you will be missing the majority of your sales. Verbally and visually you need to be able to peel back the layers and get into deeper communications, indulging in some aerobic listening to search beneath the skin. Your visual listening affirmations will be important, adding integrity and credibility to the scenario.

4. Telling

This is the bit that all salespeople adore, so much so that they will cheerily launch into the 'tell' before going through the vital stages of ear and eye listening. But you need to know what the customer wants first, so you can match their needs to your product's benefits.

The 'tell' may involve presenting, persuading, face-to-face or even telephone communication. All involve bodytalk techniques.

5. Selling

Many people can talk about a product or service, but few can actually sell it, and then go on selling it if the client relationship is to be developed. Embarrassment often makes us scupper the deal, ducking out at the end of the negotiation when we should be blowing the ink dry on the contract. Clients will display visual and verbal barriers and it is up to you to keep the dialogue open throughout to lead to the close at the end.

The word 'oh' is valuable in these types of discussion. The client makes a point and the salesperson replies: 'Oh?' to find out more information. This can be visual as well as verbal. It can be signalled subtly, with maintained eye contact, a slight eye-widening and a raise of the eyebrows, or more forcefully, with a single or double palms-up gesture and a slight shake of the head. You can also maintain your listening silence, but lean forward onto your elbows. This pose is difficult to meet without add-on communication.

6. Reviewing

Never ever fail to review your own performance, otherwise assumption and arrogance will scupper any future success. 'Watch' your own body language in retrospect and watch that of the client, too. Now you know the outcome, work out the prime moments of the meeting. Did their attitude change at any stage? Did you do enough to cope with that change and steer it? Did you have to achieve complete momentary cut-off at all, to break a negative atmosphere or tension? How was that received if you did?

This 'safe' period after the sale is also the time to build the client relationship. Once you have sold your product or service the tension evaporates and there is a 'trust time' that you should capitalise on to increase rapport and learn useful information.

Great Sale

Confidence is the key to good selling. If you can admit to selling without having a fit of the vapours, that is a good start. Preparation will also give you confidence. You need to know your product, know your objective at each transaction and know as much about your customer as possible. You need to prepare yourself, too. If the thought of selling makes you cringe, work first on your confidence levels. Look back over Chapter 2 and boost your charisma!

Selling without the small-talk is like sex without foreplay. It is bad-mannered, thoughtless and impatient. You may get what you want on a one-off occasion, but you have built no framework for a more fruitful relationship. So, start off by learning more about the client. This calls for both verbal and listening skills. Make some small-talk and then listen to the customer. That way you can learn more about them and work out how your product can benefit them.

I recently went into a mobile phone shop to buy a new model. The assistant listened while I told her my old one had broken and then proceeded with her sales pitch. She showed me one that had just come onto the market (I never ever learnt how to master my old one) and told me that it was lightweight. (I liked the feel of the other one in my hand. It was heavier and I felt less likely to drop it.) She told me it would fit into a breast pocket (which women rarely have) and that it would adapt to the Internet (not a feature I was interested in). What I wanted was a flip-front model that did nothing else other than work as a phone. What she should have done was ask open questions and then listen.

Begin, then, by a display of listening body language. Your pose can be high or low-status listening, depending on the person you are dealing with and the product you are selling. Mirror, as well. If your client is crossed or defensive, begin your own pitch in slightly similar style. If they are quiet, keep your own voice down.

If they use little eye contact, don't challenge them with your own.

When people buy they want to satisfy two sets of needs: emotional and logical. The logical ones are the easiest to deal with – if your product does the job and comes in at a suitable price, that should be the contract stitched up. But then there are the emotional aspects of the deal. Clients like the MMFI ('Make me feel important') factor in any transaction. So, never look higher in status, more relaxed or more confident than your customer. Avoid high-status displays like:

• head-tilting (backwards, chin up)
• finger-steepling
• putting your hands behind your head
• taking your jacket off without asking
• using the client's desk
• rocking your chair
• moving in too close
• crossing one leg over the other, ankle on thigh
• leaning over your client
• sitting in a much larger chair
• smoking without asking
• using more eye contact
• talking while looking out of the window or writing
• using more space or territory
• interrupting, either visually or verbally.

On the other hand, avoid overblown 'pleasing signals' like:

• hand-wringing
• stooping towards the client all the time
• over-smiling
• laughing in an exaggerated way at all the customer's funny lines
• overdone mirroring and responses
• looking horrified when the client describes a minor misfortune
• agreeing to everything that is said.

Overdone signals leave the client feeling you are being insincere.

Monitor your client's responses throughout your meeting and be ready with a response of your own. If their arms begin to cross or stay stubbornly closed, hand them a document to open them up. If you feel you have reached deadlock, think about closing down altogether. Ask if you both need to break for some tea. Change the subject. Divert attention. Get them into 'buy' mode again, even if it's not your product they're buying into at that point, but just a coffee or a chat about the news. Lead them back to the sale when you feel things are going your way again.

Another way to 'break' is to change your style of delivery. Perhaps you can pause for an 'honesty' break. I have one colleague who will suddenly announce: 'God, you're being hard work today, what's up?' This usually prompts the client to laugh and be more relaxed about raising objections.

Another technique to alter the mood of a meeting when it is going down trash alley is the small accident. A rattling tea cup, a dropped bag, a dropped pen, a couple of coins falling out of the pocket – any of these will give a sudden excuse to break from the proceedings. You apologise and the client reassures you and possibly helps you retrieve the pen. You have both functioned on a more human level. This type of stunt can break down as many barriers as the handshake or the small-talk.

Finally, with a 'buy' decision, the tension goes. The customer's body language will change so much they will almost change shape in front of your eyes. Features soften, frowns go, shoulders become less slumped. There is a visible sense of relief.

Reassurance is important at this stage. The customer wants to know that you aren't just turning on the charm until the deal is done. So, be friendly. But lay the foundations for further business. Lie back and have a cigarette by all means, but do it while you arrange the next date.

When you finally make your exit, be smooth. Rush packing up and dashing off will make it look as though you can't wait to get away now you've roped another sucker.

▶ Personal Styles

As a general rule of thumb remember that people often like people who are like them. In business this is even more true than in social life, because we have so little time to master difficult bonding. Therefore it is useful to have a greater understanding of the four main behavioural styles. Each comes with its own symptomatic body language. This makes it easier to tailor your own bodytalk to be more empathetic.

Standard psychometric tests use different names for different types. I'm going to run with my own:

1. Excitables

These people like talking and enjoy face-to-face communication. They like being the centre of attention in most situations, although they can be shy at social occasions. They like humour and entertainment and are easily bored. They hate anything mundane or repetitive. They tend to move a lot when they talk and illustrate points with generous emphatic gestures. They respond quickly to people, so your initial impact is vital. Always look pleased to see them and maintain positive-looking body language throughout the meeting. Show energy and enthusiasm for both your ideas and theirs. Freshness and innovation are important to this type. Never look too cynical or stale and avoid going into too much detail, as they will tend to be sold on the originality or excitement of an idea. They can be starters, rather than finishers, though. Expect initial enthusiasm but a general dwindling as time goes by.

2. Competitors

These people like power and status and work better if given authority and complete control. Their language is concise and to the point and they appreciate the same qualities in others. They are impatient and do not suffer fools gladly. They like ideas which add to their own personal profile in the company or which put them ahead of competitors. They can be brusque and tactless at times. Cut to the quick when you deal with them, though avoid challenging their authority or doing anything that may make them lose face. Respond quickly but be thorough as well. They specialise in asking direct questions and catching people out.

Never employ gestures or expressions that are unnecessary or suggest you are time-wasting or not being serious. Hand gestures should be emphatic and eye contact needs to be assertive. Move quickly, but without rushing. Avoid verbal and visual waffle.

3. Planners

These people are logical rather than emotional thinkers and like to be supplied with facts, figures and data. They also like the historical approach, being told where else the plan has worked or who else bought the product in the past. They need time and space to come to a decision, so avoid any sign of pressurising them. Take a while to come back with your own written proposals or outlines, if necessary, for if you rush them through they will often believe you have been slipshod. When you take a seat, manoeuvre yourself into a position that looks confident and comfortable and move very little from then on. Gestures should be calm and not exaggerated. The palms-down, open-armed approach will work well. Avoid jerky or excitable movements. Show intense listening skills. Nod a lot and never interrupt.

4. Carers

These people have relationship-based values. They like working with others as part of a team. They will be mainly motivated by the good of the group or the staff and will also be very aware of client welfare. Your personal approach will be important. Obtain rapport as soon as possible by being friendly and open. Keep notes about their kids and out-of-work interests. Ask them for help when possible. Never consider them a pushover, though. They are very suspicious of fawning approaches, can be stubborn when pushed and can suffer from a very thin skin. So avoid any gestures that show conflict or disagreement. Your body language should look honest and approachable. A sincere smile is vital and so is a warm greeting. Accept offers of coffee and eat a biscuit.

Now, you may or may not be able to classify the person you are dealing with. Your transactions may be too speedy to gain a clear insight. But perhaps you can get clues. Very few people fall totally into one category anyway. But you may get the idea of a dominant style. Also, you will hopefully have spotted your own.

Stay in your style, but learn to be flexible. Tailor your behaviour to appeal to other types. If you are talking to a group of mixed styles, then study your pitch or presentation and make sure there is something in there for everyone.

Imagine the Carer turning up at a company of Competitors, dressed in a Laura Ashley floral, with a bundle of notes under her arm. She takes a while to set up and apologises for being rather nervous, only her father is rather ill and she has had to spend the night in the hospital. She smiles at everyone and goes round introducing herself individually to all the clients. She gets rather upset when one is too busy on her mobile. When she talks about her product she emphasises the positive effect it will have on staff morale. Her talk overruns, but she felt it was worthwhile reading out that letter of thanks from the employee of a client company hundreds of miles away.

You can see how vital that behavioural alteration can be.

Key Points in a Nutshell

▶ Tailor your bodytalk to be in keeping with the culture of the business you work in.

▶ Never assume you know what the customer will find appropriate – put yourself in their place and see what will work.

▶ Avoid patronising clients or turning anger or complaint into rage.

▶ Don't be a salesperson in denial.

▶ Create immediate rapport.

▶ Listen to the customer.

▶ Study their behavioural profile and adjust your approach accordingly.

Chapter 18

*O*ff-piste: Business Bodytalk Outside the Office

I T's NOT JUST at work that we can make a lasting impression. It's often those little moments when we think we are 'off-piste' and can let our hair down. Actually, nothing in business should be considered off-piste. You are patently stupid if you think there are times when any bad behaviour will be magically deleted from the corporate memory.

This isn't being prudish, it's just being practical. I've seen too many party animals wake to regret their little lad/ladette-fest the following morning and spend the following six months clad in a corporate hair shirt. Have fun by all means, only don't risk that glittering career.

Danger zones or potential profile-raisers crop up throughout the corporate year with frightening regularity. Here are some brief survival tips.

▶ Training Courses

- ▶ Get to each session on time.

- ▶ Sit near the front. Trainers will assume you are keen and pick on you less. Don't go near the back because this looks like an effort to exclude yourself from proceedings.

▶ Make your entrance look positive.

▶ Take a couple of good pens and a good-quality notebook.

▶ Introduce yourself to the other delegates as soon as possible.

▶ Display good listening signals.

▶ Speak up as soon as possible on interactive sessions. The longer you wait, the harder it is to join in.

▶ Ask the trainer at least one question in the first two hours.

▶ Keep your body language looking positive. Never slump, fidget or sit with arms folded.

▶ In course exercises, take the role of encourager and manager, rather than displaying your virtuosity. Most course exercises are supposed to illustrate the role of a team-player. Enhance your promotion prospects by showing them who makes a good boss.

▶ Never look or sound negative. If you disagree with something, challenge in a positive manner. If you dislike the course, join in for the duration and offer positive comments, along with the critical.

▶ Position yourself on the course to reflect the way you would like to be positioned in your company.

▶ Network with the other delegates. A prime objective with most training is to break down barriers between departments.

▶ If the course is residential you may be expected to complete programmes in the evening. Tell yourself at the start that you will get tired and possibly stretched both physically and emotionally. Be professional at all times and if the delegates begin to get tired and tetchy, always keep silent, rather than joining in the battle.

▶ There is usually quite a lot of free booze on offer. Never look as though the prospect of free food and drink fills you with delight, because this looks cheap and greedy. Never get caught stuffing your face. Never take a pocketful of sweets off the table, a bottle of wine from dinner or anything that is supplied in your room. If you have a reputation as the mini-bar kid, offer to pay for this personally when settling your bill, along with any personal phone calls.

▶ Be polite to the hotel staff. An old saying runs: 'You can tell more about a man from the way he treats his servants than the way he behaves towards his equals.' Hotel staff are never servants, but you get my gist.

▶ Roll with it. If problems occur on the course, or there are personality clashes, be seen to be taking it in your stride.

▶ Build a good visible profile. Your body language should reflect drive, energy and stamina. Displaying your capacity for being positive is more valuable than your capacity for tequila sunrise.

▶ Show off your social skills alongside your business brawn. You are on show for the entire course. People will see you eating, drinking and socialising. Do check up on your table manners.

▶ Look like a professional traveller. Most promotions entail not just business/social skills, but also the ability to travel to client locations and arrive looking fresh as a daisy. Never bowl up looking harassed and lugging six carrier bags and a suitcase. Never complain about the difficult journey. Pack like a professional:

- Take a hanging suit rack for your clothes.
- Pack shoes in bags to prevent scuffs.
- Take a tube or small spray of shoe polish.
- Fold clothes around layers of tissue to prevent creasing.
- If a garment has creased, hang it in the bathroom and run the shower on hot for a few minutes, to steam out the creases.
- Pack ties in a tie-travel case.
- Pack small or sample sizes of grooming gear and make-up.
- Take your own travel alarm clock.
- Phone the hotel in advance and ask if they supply hair dryers and if there is a hotel pool.
- Pack twice as much underwear and a quarter fewer outfits than you think you will need.

- Check whether dress is smart business or casual. If it is casual, never go scruffy.
- Take a dry-clean spray, in case of accidents.
- Only use the trouser-press when you are sober or you will emerge the next morning looking as though you have been trying to turn your trousers into a fan.
- Take a good clothes brush.
- Take nightwear, even if you normally sleep in the buff. It has been known for delegates to arrive to find they're sharing rooms.

▶ Business Lunches

- ▶ Dress appropriately for the restaurant. Some places still insist on a tie.

- ▶ Book a good seat. Avoid hosting clients at the one next to the toilets or kitchens.

- ▶ Arrive on time, or much earlier if you are hosting.

- ▶ Make a favourable comment about the venue if you are being hosted. Never mention the fact that you use it regularly.

- ▶ Allow your guest to sit with their back to the wall. If you are hosting more than three people, try to find a restaurant with a round table.

- ▶ Unless the food is absolutely rancid, never complain.

- ▶ If you do need to complain, mention the problem quietly. Never sit turning your nose up and making a great visual show of disgust.

- ▶ Offer your guest the option of every course on the menu.

- ▶ If they choose one of each, do the same. Never leave your guest eating while you sit waiting.

- ▶ Be nice to the waiter.

- ▶ If you know the waiter, introduce them to your guest.

- Be territorially polite. Never place anything on your guest's side of the table.

- Never ask to try your guest's food.

- Never tell stories about your hernia operation or your dog's latest outbreak of mange.

- Never take your shoes off under the table.

- Never order by clicking your fingers.

- If service is slow, leave the table and explain to the waiter that you have to get back to the office.

- Allow your guest to order first from the menu. Most waiters will take the first and main course from each person in one go. Return the menus immediately.

- Never pick the most expensive dish or the dearest wine when you are being hosted.

- If you are a woman hosting a man, let the waiter know this discreetly.

- Tip if there is no service charge. Some credit card bills come untotalled. You are supposed to add your own tip.

- Thank your host for the meal and write a formal thank-you letter the next day.

- Don't smoke unless your guest does.

▶ The Office Party

- Don't get drunk, or even nearly drunk.

- Don't wear a party hat and stand in front of a camera or video.

- Don't bare vast expanses of flesh that normally stay under wraps during working hours.

- Don't flirt after a few drinks.

- Don't make long speeches.

- Don't drink the punch – stick to what you know.

- Knock on office doors before you go in.

- If there is a disco, be discreet when you have to shout in your colleagues' ears. The bit about the boss's wife looking like a right slapper is always yelled out just at the moment the record stops.

- Practise your dancing in front of the mirror before you go. No one is expecting you to look like one of Steps, but too many people end up looking like a constipated elephant.

- Never talk business.

- If you take a partner, brief them and then have their mouth sealed with SuperGlue. Never let them berate the boss for all that unpaid overtime or lack of promotion you so obviously deserve. Keep them off the alcohol. Buy a bottle of champagne on the way home as a reward for good behaviour.

- Never suck up to the boss's partner. Be charming but keep your distance. They have loose tongues, too. Once they've confided their spouse's pet name to you, Mr Wobbles might not be so keen to have you on the payroll.

Opting out of the office party is one way of ensuring your reputation stays intact. But you may come across looking like a party-pooper. An ankle bandage is a good gambit to get you through one year, at least. This assures you can attend, but politely and smilingly decline the Lambada contest and the 'Drink-your-own-weight-in-Bailey's' finals.

▶ The Leaving Party

- These are usually either boring, sad or wildly uplifting, depending on who is going. If you dislike the person leaving, don't go, otherwise you will find yourself acting like a hypocrite.

- Remember that people who are leaving will often feel the need to speak their minds. Prepare to get slaughtered during the leaving speech.

- Prepared to get bored, too. Employees who have barely spoken for 25 years will suddenly find they have a liking for long-winded public speaking

- If you are the one leaving, remember one word: dignity. Whatever the circumstances, this is not an occasion for vitriol, bitterness and revenge.
  If there has been acrimony, only ask the people you like.

- Never expect colleagues who are staying to back you up. You are no longer one of them, no matter how close the friendships.

- Speaking of which, a sad but true fact of office life is that friendships made in the workplace rarely survive very long after one person has left.

- Never use the leaving party as an opportunity to tell the leaver what you really think of them. Choose another time and another place.

- If you are making a speech about the person who is leaving, feel free to make it funny, but not hurtful. This is the moment when people want praise and affection. Always throw in some heart-warming stuff, even if it does sound corny.

- Keep your leaving party quite short. People will have shown up out of politeness and possibly affection, but you should never stretch them too far.

Key Points in a Nutshell

- ▶ No business/social event should be considered off the record.

- ▶ Plan business social events carefully. Leave nothing to chance, especially if you are hosting.

- ▶ Be positive.

- ▶ Don't get drunk.

Chapter 19

Business Sex: The Fine Art of Flirting at Work

SEX AT WORK is a fact of life. Throw any ill-assorted group of animals together and some are sure to start fancying others. In human terms the only ingredient that is missing to ensure an outbreak of passion is to make it feel naughty and even illegal. That is exactly what happens in the workplace.

The trouble with workplace affairs is that they can cause problems with the career and they do have an effect on group dynamics. There is an uneasy pecking order in most office packs. When two individual units pair off, they are often seen by the rest of the pack as one more powerful unit. This can be threatening.

This effect will always occur, even when both partners are of equal status. When one is the boss, the effect can be far more radical. It is a notoriously difficult juggling act. The person dating the boss may start to bathe in reflected power, making themselves desperately unpopular, or the couple keeps the affair discreet, leaving the rest of the staff to use their imagination when it comes to favouritism and pillow talk, or the lower-status partner tries to redress their popularity balance by complaining about the boss behind their back, just to show that it hasn't made any difference. This is obviously a danger to the relationship.

▶ Flirting

But what about the earlier stages? Relationships at work can involve splatter-gun flirting that is seen as non-predatory and (almost) non-sexual. In some company cultures everyone flirts with everyone else. It's the way they do business.

Business flirts are great to watch in action, just as long as they don't upset the dynamics of the group. Flirting at work is usually used as a flattering joke between both parties. Where it goes wrong is when one party is joking while the other is taking the signals to mean a full-scale sexual onslaught, or when one party is offended by the signals they are being sent. So, if you like to turn on the charm with your colleagues and clients, make sure you are able to read whether they get the joke or not, or it can all end in tears.

Good business flirting is very much a two-way conversation. It should always be subtle and jokey. In a way, it is an extension of charisma. It's done to make the recipient feel good. That's why it involves a certain amount of verbal flattery. Be careful, though – if the compliments are too inflated they may be seen as sarcastic. If they are too personal they could appear predatory or insulting. Again, never assume. The 'but that's how I behave with everyone' argument is a flawed one, because not everyone is the same. One person's joke is another's harassment.

Another way that the system breaks down is when one person flirts ferociously, but only with members of the opposite sex, or only with the bosses. I worked with one woman who was a nightmare of Freddie Kruger proportions towards all the women in the place, but turned into a Marilyn Monroe the minute any men were around. The effect was ghastly and alienating. The best flirts at work will often use their signals wholesale, charming and flattering everyone, regardless of age, sex or position in company. Some of the best fun-flirting I have seen has been between gay men and straight women at work.

One good factor of the workplace is that people get a chance to flirt without the signals being seen as an invitation for sex. The opportunities to do this outside the workplace are fewer. I have often seen groups of married friends flirt furiously with one another's partners, but that was a 'safe' environment. The flirting was a form of flattery to both partners in the relationship. Nobody ever moved in seriously and nobody felt threatened.

Flirting Signals

Flirting at work tends to consist of non-touch and non-territorial behaviour. It may be mild flattery, smiling or 'making eyes' at the other person, but in a non-staring, non-threatening manner, and it sometimes consists of quite tame erotic displays or posturing. Here's the flirting bodytalk:

▶ Eye contact – Genuine sexual interest is signalled by increased eye contact. Most people at work are told to increase their natural gaze intensity to display honesty and business confidence. This can look like flirting.

▶ Gaze-time – When we begin to register the initial attraction, there is a routine of very brief spells of eye contact punctuating long spells of looking away. This is because we find the other person attractive and this makes us cute and shy. I once noticed a colleague had fallen for her manager when she could no longer look him in the eye.

▶ Staring – When the couple get into a relationship they will indulge in long periods of eye-to-eye gazing. This is hard to maintain at work for obvious reasons and will usually be masked by total avoidance. Any occasional or accidental eye-gazing will be soulful or electric.

▶ Glancing – Traditional flirting means the woman keeps her chin down and tilted and gazes up at the man with doe-eyes. Princess Diana used this pose a lot and was dubbed 'Shy Di' because of it.

▶ The suppressed smile – The person will go to smile, but then either stop it with a lip-pucker or by covering the mouth with a hand.

▶ Giggling – This very childish form of laughter is supposed to register youthfulness and a shared sense of naughtiness.

- Self-touch –The flirt will touch semi-sensual areas to imply that is what they would like the viewer to do. The options for this are obviously limited in business. This is not to be confused with the male genital or bottom-touch, which is usually done either as a comfort or status gesture.

  With flirting the mouth is usually favourite, with fingers being placed near or in it, or the fingertips caressing the edge of the lips, or a tongue-licking gesture.

  The neck is a slightly more overt area, and any gentle caress – especially one that slides downward – can be a flirting signal.

  The legs can be stroked and the hair can be played with.

- Closeness – Attraction is shown through sitting or leaning a little closer to the other person than normal spatial etiquette would allow.

- Openness – Although body barriers may initially increase through shyness, attraction can be signalled through a lack of barrier gestures and sitting and standing face-on to the other person. If the legs are crossed they will tend to be crossed towards the person we are attracted to.

- Licking – The tongue may be used more, licking the lips or the fingers, or in the consumption of food. *Ally McBeal* included a famous seduction at work scene where two women licked the froth off their cappuccinos.

- Smiling – When we are attracted to someone we tend to smile and nod more when they are talking.

- Playfulness – There is a sense of puppyish fun between people who find one another attractive. There will be more use of small touches, with playful hitting, patting or punching used as 'excuse' touch and denial gestures in place of more serious touch.

- Erotic displays – In a nightclub you'd be dancing, but in the workplace it's more likely to be stretching, leaning, bending and perching on desks. Macho posturing displays include sticking out the chest, straightening the back, pulling the stomach in, etc.

- Grooming displays – Touching the hair or clothing to check it looks OK.

- Denial gestures – Wearing a short skirt and then continually tugging it down; sporting a low-cut blouse but carrying documents to cover the cleavage, etc. (I tried to think of a male version, but failed dismally.)

- Attention-seeking displays – Distance work can include loud laughter, exaggerated gestures, hair-flicking, head-tossing and leg-swinging, and possibly increased touching of friends of the same sex, mostly punctuated by glances to check that the other person is watching.

- Hair or head-tossing.

- Glancing up sideways at the colleague.

- Lowered-chin glancing, combined with a closed-mouth smile.

- For a man, hands on hips or a hand running down the tie to straighten it. Guess what – the tie is a long strip of fabric that points in a straight line towards the genitals.

- Standing close to a woman who is sitting at her desk, so that the genitals are at eye level and she is forced to look up from that level to make eye contact.

- For a woman, crossed legs with the top leg swinging slowly and a hand caressing the knee.

- Fingering the neckline of a low-cut top.

Most of the above will fall into the 'heavy-duty' category and be inappropriate in the workplace, although I have seen all of them in action at some time. The problem with many of them is that they could also happily fit under the heading of sexual harassment if the person on the receiving end found them inappropriate.

The other problem is that nearly all of the techniques above can be caused by quite innocuous, non-flirting triggers. Misreading signals can be dangerous.

Power Corrupts

Status brings its own 'misread' problems. Staff tend to be nice to bosses. It's the way of the world. This person has power over your money and your future career. And so you are polite, helpful, friendly, and maybe even flirty.

Any boss with one ounce of brain cell would understand that most of this behaviour has been prompted by the power factor. The vain and the egotistic, however, start to believe that it is not only because of their job title but because along with their promotion to management they became drop-dead gorgeous. The delusion can be dangerous. Some start comparing their PAs to partners and then wondering why the person at home can't be so tuned into their every need, and respectful and helpful and dressed all the time in Armani.

Turn-offs

Hopefully you will never push the flirting boundaries too far but if you do, don't always assume the other person will either tell you or send hints via their behaviour. When people get embarrassed, as they often do in cases of inappropriate sexual behaviour, their visual signalling will often veer towards denial. Illogical though it may be, we will often end up representing agreement or collusion. So, the person on the receiving end may smile to mask their discomfort or laugh and even join in. This is the survival response. When cornered by something we dislike, we sometimes mirror or play along, rather than fight our corner.

When the complaint goes in later, the response is often: 'If you didn't like it you should have told me at the time.' The point is that we often don't like to.

Threats

The most threatening sexual displays at work will often come from the stare, proximity and, obviously, touch. Eye contact is a potent signaller and so is spatial intrusion. Either can be used in a way that would be threatening to anyone. Touch is less sinuous.

We each have unwritten rules about who can touch us and where. In business the only 'normal' touch is the handshake, with the addition of a brief touch on the arm or shoulder if someone is deeply distressed. Closer work friendships or less formal work cultures may mean more variations. But these variations have to be allowed. Telling colleagues you are a tactile person and then running rampage is not appropriate. If you are a naturally tactile person you will need to tone that down for business. Your upbringing is not an excuse.

Dating Procedures

Probably the best way to get a date with a colleague is to be open about your intentions, but only with the person you intend dating. The problem with the workplace is in the misread signal. This worry can lead to 'long-elastic' chat-ups, where banter goes on but no one wants to take the big step of declaring their intentions because a refusal will not only offend, but may well be devastating.

Pride is a big problem. At work there is no hiding-place. If you ask out someone you meet casually at a social event you know there is no need to cross paths again if the answer is no. If your colleague turns you down, though, you have to keep face – which needless to say isn't easy. This is where the 'I was only joking' umbilical cord comes in.

E-mail is seen as a way of 'I was only joking' flirting. Face-to-face banter can go on for what seems like forever. A business dinner can be claimed to be just that. Everything short of sex itself can be an 'I was only joking' gesture (although sometimes even sex can be dismissed the next day as 'nothing serious').

The confusion will cause problems for the one on the receiving end, as well. When do you say 'no thanks'? When does harmless flirting become more serious? When is a late supper a date, rather than working late? Unlike social encounters, the margins become heavily blurred in business. It's as well to be aware of what you are really aiming for with any flirtatious behaviour.

Key Points in a Nutshell

- ▶ Flirting at work can be fun and a useful method of communication.

- ▶ Misreading signals can be dangerous. Keep the communication two-way at all times.

Conclusion

BODY LANGUAGE CAN be a fun topic for parties, but business is a more serious matter. Remember this book is not a book of tricks. I have tried to provide a fast-track handbook for working people, but you should never underestimate or over-simplify the process.

Apart from the more distinct signals, like giving someone the finger or a V-sign, nearly every gesture or expression you make or receive can – like most words in the English language – have many different translations. To give a word proper meaning you place it in a sentence and align it with other words. You give the word tonal emphasis. The same applies to your body language 'words'. You need to read them in context. You need to balance them with the other signals the eye and the ear receive. Even quick decisions need to be taken based on all the information available.

So, when you 'speak' in bodytalk, take the time to ensure you say the right things. Know your audience and know your desired message and use gestures, expression and posture to relay that message in a congruent, credible way.

Enjoy putting into practice what you have read in this book, but never underestimate its power or its complexity.

*I*ndex

Note: Page numbers in italics refer to illustrations.

Piatkus Business Books

PIATKUS BUSINESS BOOKS have been created for people like you, whether you are busy executives and managers or just starting your career. They provide expert knowledge in a clear and easy-to-follow format. All the books are written by specialists in their field. They will help you improve your skills quickly and effortlessly in the workplace and on a personal level. They are available in all good bookshops or by visiting our website at www.piatkus.co.uk

The 10-Day MBA: A step-by-step guide to mastering the skills taught in top business schools   Steven Silbiger

10-Minute Time And Stress Management: How to gain an 'extra' 10 hours a week!   Dr David Lewis

Brain Power: The 12-week mental training programme
Marilyn vos Savant & Leonore Fleischer

Careershift: How to plan and develop a successful career
Bridget Wright

The Complete Book of Business Etiquette: The essential guide to getting ahead in business   Lynne Brennan & David Block

The Complete Conference Organisers Handbook Robin Connor

The Complete Time Management System: Change the way you work and 'save' 2 hours a day! Christian H. Godefroy & John Clark

Confident Public Speaking: How to communicate successfully using the PowerTalk system Christian Godefroy & Stephanie Barrat

Continuous Quality Improvement: A hands-on guide to setting up and sustaining a cost-effective quality programme Alasdair White

Corporate Charisma: How to achieve world-class recognition by maximising your company's image, brands and culture Dr Paul Temporal & Dr Harry Alder

Dealing With Difficult People: Proven strategies for handling stressful situations and defusing tensions Roberta Cava

The Engaged Customer: The new rules of Internet Direct Marketing Hans Peter Brondmo

Enterprise One to One: Tools for building unbreakable customer relationships in the information age Don Peppers & Martha Rogers

The Essential Guide to Developing Your Staff: How to recruit, train, coach and mentor top-quality people Alasdair White

Financial Know-how for Non-financial Managers: Easy ways to understand accounts and financial planning John Spencer and Adrian Puss

Getting Everything You Can Out of All You've Got: 21 ways you can out-think, out-perform and out-earn the competition Jay Abraham

Grow Rich with peace of mind Napoleon Hill

How to Survive Without a Job: Practical solutions for developing skills and building self-esteem Ursula Markham

Quantum Learning for Business: Discover how to be more effective, confident and successful at work Bobbi DePorter with Mike Hernacki

Reinventing Leadership: Strategies to empower the organisation Warren Bennis & Robert Townsend

The Right Brain Manager: How to use the power of our mind to achieve personal and professional success Dr Harry Alder

The Right Way to Write: How to write effective letters, reports, memos and e-mails Rupert Morris

Say What You Mean and Get What You Want George R. Walther

Secrets of Successful Interviews: Tactics and strategies for winning the job you really want Dorothy Leeds

Speak for Yourself: The complete guide to effective communication and powerful presentations Cristina Stuart

The Ten Second Internet Manager: Survive, thrive and drive your company in the Information Age Mark Breier

Total Memory Workout: 8 easy steps to maximum memory fitness Cynthia R. Green

Train Your Brain: The ultimate 21 day mental skills programme for peak performance Dr Harry Alder

What Will Be: How the new world of information will change our lives Michael Dertouzos

The Working Woman's Handbook: The essential reference guide for every working woman Polly Bird

Workshift: How to survive and thrive in the workplace of the future Sue Read